# THE RAIN DANCE PEOPLE

The Pueblo Indians, their past and present

## by RICHARD ERDOES

ALFRED A. KNOPF · NEW YORK

*All photographs in this book are by Richard Erdoes, with the exception of the following, for which grateful acknowledgement is made.* Budnik, page 7. Jaki Erdoes, pages 43, 261. Cyril Griffin, page 258. Museum of the American Indian, Heye Foundation, page 206. New Mexico State Tourist Bureau, page 245. Camilla Smith, pages 152, 201, 211, 213, 215, 216 (1), 248 (1), 251, 254, 256, 262, 271. Smithsonian Institution National Anthropological Archives, Bureau of American Ethnology Collection, pages 26, 44, 55, 83, 142, 145, 147, 150, 158, 176, 181, 189, 193, 204, 208, 219, 223, 228. U.S. Department of the Interior, Bureau of Indian Affairs, page 22. U.S. Department of the Interior, Bureau of Reclamation, page 51 (3 and 4).

THIS IS A BORZOI BOOK PUBLISHED BY ALFRED A. KNOPF, INC.

*Library of Congress Cataloging in Publication Data*

Erdoes, Richard.   The rain dance people.
Summary: Traces the history of the Pueblo Indians and discusses their present government, customs, art, way of life, and relationship to the white man and his government.
1. Pueblo Indians—Juvenile literature.
[1. Pueblo Indians.  2. Indians of North America]
I. Title.   E99.P9E72     1975     973'.04'97     74–157
ISBN 0–394–82394–X ISBN 0–394–92394–4 lib. bldg.
0 9 8 7 6 5 4 3 2 1

# CONTENTS

# THE RAIN DANCE PEOPLE

# 1 ▪ THE LAND OF WHITE RADIANCE

*We were told by Masauwu,*
*The Creator: "This is your*
*Land. Keep it for me until*
*I come back."*

THOMAS BENYACYA, HOPI ELDER

Perched on a high rock rising abruptly from the surrounding plain, an Indian village can be seen. The rock is so huge that it makes the houses, built of adobe bricks and mud, look like toys. The village is old. It was old when Columbus landed on the shores of the New World. But it is only the last in a chain of cities the people who settled on this rock had built, reaching far back through the ages into prehistory.

An old woman is sitting at the edge of the cliff, her eyes taking in all the land: the arid plain dotted with cornfields and herds of grazing sheep, the multicolored mesas, and the distant mountain ranges half hidden in the bluish haze. "You want to know how this earth and the creatures living upon it came to be," says the woman, "this land which you Anglos call the Southwest. The land is old, so old that human words and numbers are inadequate to describe its great age. It is a land of gods and humans who are part of this earth. This is what my grandmother told me, as she had been told when she was a small child. There was a world before this one, below the surface of the earth. In that long-ago world the Corn Mother worked many wonders. She gave names to all things, and in time, after she named them, those things became real. The sun and the moon became real. The stars and the rainstorms and the Kachinas, the friendly spirits who make it rain. When all was finally ready, after many lifetimes as we count them, Iatik, the mother, thought it time to put out her children.

Santana Antonio, of Acoma, New Mexico, has many legends to tell her grandchildren, tales of another world which existed long before the one we live in now, a universe beneath the surface of the earth, from which the first people emerged into our world.

"And so the people came out from the earth through the hole of emergence called Sipapu at our sacred mountain far away to the north. You can just barely see it from here. They crawled into our world soft, naked, and helpless like grasshoppers. They were blind like newborn mice. Iatik lined them up in a row facing east and made the sun come up for the first time in this new world to shine upon them. And when its rays shone upon the eyes of the people, they were opened and they could see. Even nowadays, when a baby is born, we go to the edge of the cliff and lift it up to be kissed by the rays of the morning sun.

"There was a lake on top of the mountain near the place of emergence. Iatik put the first people on an island in the middle of the lake. She taught them how to fend for themselves, how to look for food, how to grow corn. She told them about the gods called

Kachinas which dwell in a place called Wenimats. She taught them how to make prayer sticks and how to dance for rain, because without rain there can be no life. Each pueblo has its own way of telling this story. We might differ a little on this point or that, but we all say that there was a world before this one and that people and animals came up from it through a hole of emergence which is right here, somewhere, in the Southwest. And though we Pueblo tribes speak different languages, we all call this place Sipapu or something that sounds very much like it. And we all have prophecies which say that this world of today could vanish in the flash of a moment as the one before unless we lead good, natural lives, treating the earth as sacred, as a part of us. Well, that is what we say."

The earth, then, is a land of gods and humans, animals and plants, all depending on one another. It is an ever-changing land. Through eons of time oceans came and went, covering the earth and the mountains for the space of one geological age or the other, receding again, leaving the fossilized remains of shells and other creatures of the sea embedded in the many-colored layers of deep canyon walls. Mountains rose up, eroded, and disappeared. Dinosaurs came, leaving huge, three-toed tracks in the red sandstone of Navajo Land, disappearing when their time had passed. With them disappeared the dense forests which once covered the Southwest giving nourishment to the great reptiles who had grown too big for their environment. The forests left their bones in the shape of giant petrified tree trunks strewn over the painted desert, trunks which in the course of untold years turned into agate and crystal, into opalizing hues of vermilion and purple.

Forever the land was changing—from ocean to forest to desert to prairie. As the great reptiles vanished, the mammals thrived. Among the bigger animals were the giant ground sloth, the long-necked camel, the woolly rhinoceros, and the shaggy mammoth. Herds of bison, much larger than the buffalo of today, dotted the plains.

Some 150 million years ago a lumbering dinosaur left his three-toed footprint in the red Arizona sandstone.

Finally human beings arrived. We do not know when. Until recently it was thought that the first humans appeared on our continent about twenty-five thousand years ago, but recent discoveries are pushing this date back farther and farther. In California human remains and crude artifacts found in the 1970s are thought to be much older. The two-legged newcomers still found the mammoth roaming the prehistoric plains, and they hunted it. Beautifully worked, fluted spearheads of stone—so-called Folsom points—have been found embedded in the bones of long-extinct bisons. These skillfully made weapons tell us that the Native Americans of ten thousand years ago had already reached a high stage of human development.

Some anthropologists say that the people we misnamed "Indians," because Columbus and his men thought at first they had landed in India, came to this continent by way of a landbridge that once connected the Aleutian Islands. Others think that they traveled from Asia to America over the ice of the frozen Bering Strait. All are agreed that the First Americans originally came from Northeast Asia, making the crossing in the Arctic regions where the continents almost touch, pressing forever southward in their search for game.

The migrations might have occurred in a few great waves or in a steady trickle, but within a few thousand years—a comparatively short time in the long history of humankind—these nomads spread over two continents, from Alaska to the southernmost tip of South America.

Many Indians do not share this view. "We have always been here," they say. "Maybe we are the ones who traveled West and populated Asia." The Norwegian explorer Thor Heyerdahl showed that the traffic could have gone the other way when he sailed westward from Peru to Tahiti in his Indian-type balsa raft *Kon Tiki*.

However that may be, a migration from Siberia to Alaska is the most widely accepted view. The Indian and Mongolian races are obviously related; Japanese travelers in the Southwest are often taken for Navajos. A young Pueblo friend and I were once in a Korean restaurant where the smiling owner greeted him in the Korean language, saying over and over, "Surely you must be one of us." Art forms such as pottery and pottery decoration, which arose in the same historical period simultaneously in China and South America, are so similar that it is unlikely to be the result of pure coincidence. Whether the original migration traveled from Asia to America, or vice versa, at times there was human contact, however fragile, between the two continents.

The nomads who drifted into the Southwest considered themselves lucky. The land they chose for their home was beautiful, and generation after generation they clung to it with a fierce, enduring love that has lasted to our time. It has been called the Land of Turquoise Skies, the Land of Enchantment, the Land Where Time Stands Still. It is a land of dazzling light and deep shadows. An old Indian chant says, "I see the Earth, I am looking down upon her and smile, because this makes me happy. And the Earth, looking back at me, is smiling too. May I walk happily and lightly upon her."

The Four Corners region is among the most spectacular in this country, the location of many national parks and monuments. This is Monument Valley, part of the Navajo reservation. The area is dotted with ruins and rock paintings left by the ancestors of the modern Pueblos.

It is a land of contrasts—of high, snow-capped mountain ranges and flat, arid prairies; a region of innumerable buttes and mesas—natural tabletops rising abruptly from immense plains. They do not rise by accident, say the Indians. They believe that the land and all living things upon it are bound in one eternal circle of life. It is a land where rivers, mountains, and lakes take on an almost human

Not all of the Southwest is arid brush country. Snow-capped mountain ranges hide cool lakes encircled by meadows and forests. This is the sacred Blue Lake of the Taos people; after a long struggle, it has been returned to them by the U.S. goverment.

quality. They become "enchanted," magic places, the subjects of songs and legends—as well as the objects of prayers.

This is also a region of deserts with a strange and haunting beauty of their own. To the uninitiated a desert is silent and dead; yet it teems with hidden life. Those who know it, animals and humans, can draw sustenance from it. Forbidding-looking barrel cacti are natural containers of sweet, refreshing liquids to quench a wanderer's thirst. Nor is the desert always waterless. A sudden flash flood can transform it almost overnight into a meadow of wildflowers. The crisp, dry desert air has powers to heal. Many victims of tuberculosis have been cured by it.

There are sacred lakes in the Southwest, such as the Blue Lake of the Taos Indians, which was recently returned to them after a long struggle. These lakes are places for pilgrimages and worship; clean springs serve as shrines in which white shells and turquoise are thrown as prayers for future blessings. The slopes of the high mountains are covered with Douglas fir, juniper, and Ponderosa pine. Here women gather pine nuts in baskets, never taking too much but leaving enough for the squirrels and other four-legged creatures. At their work the women are watched by the mountain lion, all-seeing but seldom seen.

The Southwest contains many of North America's natural wonders—the Grand Canyon, Canyon de Chelly, Mesa Verde, Monu-

The saguaro cactus is typical in some Arizona deserts.

For centuries, animals and humans dwelling in harmony with the land have drawn sustenance from it.

ment Valley, the Petrified Forest, the Painted Desert, Rainbow Bridge, Saguaro National Monument, the Great Sand Dunes, Organ Pipe Cactus National Monument, and many more. Working this land is not easy; the people must struggle to wrest a living from it. Maybe it is all the more precious to them for that reason. Summer days can be frightfully hot, though the nights are always cool. Winters can be harsh and cold, a time of icy blizzards. In 1972 snowdrifts isolated many Navajo communities, and food and medicine had to be flown to them by helicopters. But over the centuries the Indians have adapted to this earth, as the land has to them. For

Once, millions of years ago, the desert country of the Southwest was covered with lush forests and grassland that were populated by the mammoth, the woolly rhinoceros, the camel, and the giant ground sloth. The people who have lived in this land for untold generations have adapted themselves to the changing landscape.

generations it has nourished the Indian with game, corn, squash, and beans for food. It has yielded up grasses and reeds for baskets, fibers for mats and clothing, herbs to cure sicknesses, clay for pottery vessels, wood and stone for artifacts, adobe mud for dwellings, and turquoise for adornments. Little wonder, then, that many Indians look upon this land as their mother, the center of this universe.

Thomas Benyacya, a Hopi elder who represented the Indian point of view before the United Nations in New York and at the International Conference on the Environment in Stockholm, Sweden, said: "Once all mankind was one and in harmony with its surroundings. Then our white brother separated from us and went east, across the great waters. It was said that at some time he would come back with all his great inventions to help his red brother and then we would be as one again. But our white brother misunderstood and misused his inventions which ruin the land which he no longer knows and understands. We still hope that Bahana, our white brother, will come back to us to bring peace instead of war, peace to men and peace to the earth. Here, in the four corners, we Indians still cling to our old ways, our traditions, our rites, our prophesies, our way of life. We think that for this reason this land, the Four Corners Area of southern Utah and Colorado, of Arizona and New Mexico, could one day become a last refuge for mankind where a few people of goodwill could start all over again healing and remaking this earth, because here is the center, the Holy Place of Emergence."

In the land of the Southwest Indians, rain is all-important. If the rains fail, everything fails; life comes to a stop. All religion, all prayers, ceremonies, and dances of the Southwest Indians are essentially prayers for rain, for the waters that will make the sacred corn grow and enable humans, animals, and plants to live and multiply. This is why some call the Native Americans of this region the Rain Dance People.

# 2 ▪ THE MAMMOTH HUNTERS

*A translucent, beautifully veined
piece of stone, beautifully and
delicately fashioned—they left
us nothing else, but by this we
know them.*

CHARLES LUMMIS

Human beings came to the Southwest a long time ago, as anthropologists will tell us. Scientists might also point to the ruins of an ancient city and say, "These cliff dwellings were abandoned in the year twelve hundred, for lack of water." Or they could examine mummified human remains and remark, "This man died exactly eight hundred and twelve years ago."

How do they know? Are they guessing or talking through their hats? In fact, they know exactly what they are about, and we can accept their findings with confidence. Scientists can establish the age of prehistoric objects, human and animal remains, or an ear of corn found in the ashes of an ancient campfire in two ways. The first is called radiocarbon dating and the second, dendrochronology, popularly known as the tree-ring method. Both were discovered and developed in the United States.

Of the two techniques, the tree-ring method has become a specialty of archaeologists working in the Southwest. An expert can tell exactly to the year the age of a tree trunk or a charred piece of wood recovered from a prehistoric site.

This is a book about live people and not about ruins and old bits of wood. But if one wants to understand the native people of the Southwest, one must know something about their history. Indians have their roots in the past in a way that cannot be easily imagined by whites. White Americans are essentially without roots; they have come from all parts of Europe. They pride themselves on their mobility, their willingness to pull up stakes at a moment's notice. Most of them change apartments and homes several times during their lives.

To the Indian this seems strange. "These people have no feeling for the earth beneath their feet," said a gray-haired Pueblo elder. "They are not even aware of it. Often they don't even know the place where their parents are buried. I feel sorry for them, but I cannot understand such people."

For whites, on the other hand, it is hard to understand the extent to which the Indian is wedded to the land and the old ways. An apt comparison might be a man of English descent who still spoke the language of the Saxon King Harold, held the same religious beliefs, kept the same customs, ate the same food, and tilled his land in the same manner as a Saxon yeoman of a thousand years ago. But such a man, if he existed, would never have left his English homestead in the first place.

For the Indian, time has moved slowly. Indian men feel the spirits of their ancestors around them. They pass on the wisdom of their people to the young, teaching them in the secrecy and semi-darkness of the kivas—the ceremonial underground chambers—the same circular kivas that we can see in the ancient cliff dwellings.

Indian women still fashion their pottery in the same way, using the same designs that their ancestors used long ago. They employ the same materials and methods to build the same kind of houses. Hunters still carry the same kind of hunting charms, and perform the same rites for a slain deer as did their forefathers.

We speak of different cultures and archaeological eras—Mogollon, Hohokam, Basket Makers or Anasazis. But each of these is not so very different from any other. One culture does not end abruptly to be displaced by one totally unrelated. Rather, one era passes on its heritage to the next which adds its share of knowledge to it— the discovery of a spear-thrower, the art of making fiber, or the

The pottery jar on the left is modern, made by Santana Antonio of Acoma barely ten years ago. The smaller pot is of prehistoric origin. Both were made in the same way with the same materials. Even the design is the same. The Indians of the Southwest cling to their ancient ways following a path their ancestors have walked before them.

use of pottery. The history of the Southwest is one of continuity, interrupted only here and there by the arrival of a backward tribe of warlike raiders, which in time is absorbed into the general pattern of life imposed by the earth, the sun, the rain, and those who have lived there before.

No wonder, then, that the Indians consider themselves but links in an unbroken chain, fragments of the circle without beginning and without end, people who derive great satisfaction and a sense of identity from the past, people for whom a few hundred years are but a minute in life's experience.

Of course, not all Indians think this way. Some young people would rather drive to town and listen to rock and roll than to an old man reciting ancient tales. Others would bring electricity and TV into their villages, even though the tribal elders frown on this, rather than practice traditional dances. This leads to a certain amount of tension. Even those who do not want change, especially when change is forced upon them from the outside, sometimes must accept it.

Hopis, who have never even acknowledged the existence of the white government and whose tradition forbids them to have anything to do with the white man's law, find themselves in court suing a coal company that wants to strip-mine their lands out of existence. Holy men, who should always stay home, travel to Washington to speak for their people. Tribes are forced to deal with land developers, dam builders, copper and uranium mining companies. This is not easy for a people who are trying desperately to hold on to their ancient ways while surrounded by the white world of highways, airplanes, telecommunications, missiles, and the strange squares of green paper called money. But hold on they must, or cease to be Indians. In their struggle they find strength and comfort in recalling their past.

What was this past like?

The beginning of the story is hidden by the mists of time. First came the hunters drifting down from the north, out of the cradle called Asia, men who did not know how to plant or to weave or to cook their food in pots. Ever following the tracks of their game, they hunted the giant beasts of the period—the mammoth, the woolly rhinoceros, wild cattle with huge horns, camels with necks like giraffes. We must admire the courage of these unknown early Americans. Their weapons were puny—primitive wooden lances with stone points, knives made of splintered bone—yet they took on the towering mammoth with its long, curved tusks, to feed their women and children. In 1951 a mammoth skeleton was found in Arizona together with eight spearheads, some of them stuck in its ribs. It took that many to kill the mighty beast. Archaeologists tell us that this particular hunt had its happy ending twelve thousand

Human beings arrived in the American Southwest many thousands of years ago when long-extinct mammoths still roamed the land. With primitive weapons they fearlessly hunted these giant beasts.

years ago. Was it happy? Seemingly, yes. Here are the well-made stone spearheads of the type experts call Clovis points and the bones of the extinct elephant, but no trace of human remains. So we can guess that a whole tribe of contented hunters feasted that day. A strange fact is worth mentioning here. Plenty of animal bones and stone weapons have been found, but no remains of those earliest hunters of the Southwest. We do not know why. Maybe they had their own special way of disposing of their dead.

Finds such as the mammoth bones with their eight Clovis points give us a tantalizing glimpse of the early hunters. They tell a story, but it is a mystery story that is only partially solved.

Lo, the poor hunter! Archaeologists have given him names that would have astounded him: Sandia man, Clovis man, Folsom man. The names all come from towns, mountain ranges, or caves where a particular site was excavated. The difference between these groups is usually the shape and size of the spear points they used—fluted, leafed, knife-shaped, lopsided. Different groups stuck to points of certain shapes for hundreds, or even thousands, of years. Some people call these points arrowheads, but they are wrong. The invention of the bow and arrow, a giant step in the development of early man in America, did not occur until between two and three thousand years ago. Also, people are puzzled at the carelessness with which the early hunters left their beautiful spear points about, forever losing or mislaying them. The answer to this puzzle was easy. Collectors of spear points and arrowheads, and those who experimented with various techniques of making them, found that once they got the knack of it they could make beautiful points in mere minutes using only simple implements of stone, wood, or bone. The early hunters were careless with their points because it was easier to make a new one than to search for one that was lost.

Some aristocrats among early stone points. The small, fluted one is a Folsom point.

The early hunters whose sites have been dug up lived between seven and fifteen thousand years ago, possibly even twenty thousand years ago. Though we have found no older sites, this does not mean that they do not exist. Most finds have been made accidentally by amateurs. The Folsom site, the discovery of which made a great stir in the press, was found by a black cowboy looking for a lost cow. He stopped chasing it long enough to investigate a few curious-looking bones sticking out of a dried-up river bank.

Because these early hunters had arrived at a fairly high stage of human development, we can be sure that others preceded them. If they did not invent the bow and arrow, they at least made two other important discoveries: they knew how to make and use fire and they invented the spear-thrower, the so-called *atlatl*. This was a grooved stick, attached to the wrist with a loop of rawhide. It made the arm thrust longer, giving it more force. It guided the spear more accurately and propelled it farther than the arm alone could. The *atlatl* got its name from the Aztecs who used it to hurl their spears at the Spanish conquistadors. It is a sophisticated tool and was in use, in various forms, for thousands of years.

Hunters in New Guinea and South America, who still use a spear-thrower like the atlatl, bring their game down at a distance of sixty or seventy feet. Looked upon in the light of human development, the invention of the atlatl required as much intelligence as the discovery of atomic power.

The mammoth hunter had a variety of tools at his disposal—needle-shaped bone awls, scrapers, spear-shaft straighteners, stone hammers, and fishhooks. He probably adorned himself according to his taste or to identify himself as a member of a certain tribe, with daubs of paint or simple ornaments made of shell or stone. He might have worn necklaces made of seeds. He was sophisticated enough to be a gambler, using bone disks or animal knucklebones for chips. He knew how to cross wide streams and even braved the

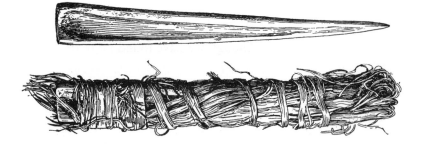

The early hunters used many bone tools—awls, needles, scrapers, borers —even knives.

This is a modern bone knife made less than a hundred years ago. It is sharp and deadly.

ocean to explore an offshore island—possibly on an inflated animal skin. He might even have discovered the advantages of specialization. In one prehistoric cave many bast-woven moccasins were discovered—hundreds of them. One could easily come to the conclusion that here was a man, an unlucky or untalented hunter, who, maybe helped by his family, made footgear for the tribe in return for a steady supply of meat.

Sometime between 6000 and 4000 B.C., the great beasts on which the early hunters relied for their food supply died out. We do not know why, but possibly it was due to a change in climate. Once the Southwest was humid, covered with moist forests and swamps. As the glaciers receded northward, the climate became hotter and drier. Plants and trees vanished, and the animals with them. This is one theory. Some scientists say that the huge beasts, never too numerous, were simply over-hunted. One way of hunting the mammoth or the giant bison was to stampede a herd of these animals over a cliff with firebrands, noise, and the waving of skin blankets. Animals that did not die outright were maimed and could be killed easily. This was the surest and least-dangerous method, but it was also wasteful. Humans and animals faced an ecological crisis. The animals could not adapt to new conditions; the humans, having better developed brains, could.

Men who had learned to live in swamplands learned to survive in the desert. They learned to go for long periods without water. They trained themselves to run down the smaller, fleet-footed desert animals. Some of the barrel-chested Apaches can still do this, and their cousins below the border, the Tarahumaras of Chihuahua, can still be seen jogging along at a steady dogtrot to visit a market town fifteen or twenty miles away. But no matter how ingeniously the mammoth hunter and primitive food-gatherer adapted to his new environment, he could no longer survive by hunting alone. He would have to find a way to raise his own food, or perish. He did not perish.

# 3 ▪ TINY COBS OF CORN

*Their secret of success was
profoundly simple: They came
to grips with, but did not abuse,
nature. They became part of the
ecological balance instead of
destroying it.*

EMIL W. HAURY

As the desert ever so slowly advanced to engulf one strip of land after another, many large mammals moved north with the receding forests, with the lush, moist pastures that nourished them. Men who could not or would not adapt to a changing environment followed the tracks of the big game inland. They left behind those who did not want to abandon the land in which they had dwelled for generations, hardy people rooted to their mesas and canyons, capable of molding themselves to the changed conditions.

Nature is a stern teacher. People surrounded on all sides by game for food, people who have only to stretch out their hands to grasp a wild fruit, have little need for new skills. The people who stayed on in the ever-drier Southwest needed to invent new ways to feed themselves. Thus, say the anthropologists, are civilizations born. Sandwiched between the primitive mammoth hunters and the later Mogollon and Hohokam civilizations are thousands of years of human development, the Age of the Cochise Culture, which derived its name from a small town in Arizona where many remains of this stage of prehistory were first dug up in 1926. Some Cochise sites were found to be eight thousand years old.

The Cochise men were primarily foragers—food-gatherers. They still did a lot of hunting, needing meat to survive. But the big animals were mostly gone. Men probably used slightly curved rabbit

Before people learned to plant corn, they had to depend largely on the gathering of wild plants and nuts. This picture shows an Indian woman using a stone pestle to grind wild acorns into a sort of flour as did her ancestors thousands of years ago.

sticks to hunt small game as the people of the Southwest have done ever since. Cochise men were not particular. If they could get nothing better, they ate snakes, lizards, or insects—and liked it. But increasingly they depended on wild plants for their food, roaming what we now call the border region in search of berries, piñon nuts, yucca fruit, grass seeds, mesquite beans, and succulent cactus plants that not only provided sweet, nourishing pulp but were also natural storage jars for liquids in time of drought.

The people clothed themselves in animal hides, rabbit furs, or materials woven of plant fibers. At first, they lived in caves and brush shelters. They had no fixed settlements; they were always on the move, combing one area  for food and then drifting on to the next. They moved in small bands because foraging cannot long support a large number of people in one place. This stage of life in the Southwest lumped together under the name Cochise culture lasted an immensely long time—from approximately 10,000 B.C. to the Christian era. Superficially life remained much the same during all this time, but in reality great developments took place. In 1948, cobs of corn, only a little more than an inch long, were found in Bat Cave, New Mexico. They were estimated to be five thousand years old. Corn is a very special plant. It does not reproduce itself from seed. It must be planted by man and cared for. To make the giant step from a mere food-gatherer to a farmer who raises his own food, to be sophisticated enough to improve one's crops by breeding, was a tremendous achievement.

"Treat your corn lovingly as you would treat your child" is an old Pueblo saying. Corn was, and still is, sacred to the people of the Southwest. It is indeed a wonderful plant. It resists extreme heat or cold. It can grow in a rain forest or in a near-desert, at sea level in the lowlands as well as in the thin air of alpine mountainsides. In time, people created thousands of varieties of corn to suit every condition and region. The Cochise people did not invent corn planting. The knowledge came to them from the south, from Mexico and Central America where corn, peppers, and pumpkins had been grown for centuries before it reached the area we associate with the Cochise culture. Farming, even at its most primitive stage, at once changed the lives of those starting to practice it. From the moment the first kernel of corn was planted, people were no longer dependent upon the luck of the hunt. Planting meant security; it meant that men and women could settle down in one place, living in the winter on corn stored in the fall in slab-lined holes dug into the sandy floors of caves. Once people discovered how to raise corn, it was an easy step to learn to plant other crops such as squash and beans. Farming also meant an increase in population. Nature somehow controls the number of people living in any given area by the amount of food available to them. A foraging or hunting family needed a few square miles to roam over in search of food. A few acres were sufficient to support a farmer.

The change did not occur from one day to the next. For centuries, rudimentary farming went hand in hand with hunting and food-gathering which, as a matter of fact, never stopped. Even today, Pueblo women will take a few days off to gather piñon nuts while their men go rabbit and deer hunting. But, in time, foraging and hunting became less and less important until they were no more than a welcome pastime to supplement one's diet. Life depended on corn. Villages grew up around cornfields. Sometime between 400 and 300 B.C., the Cochise people settled in permanent villages after having learned to breed new kinds of drought-resisting corn.

Once people settled down in one place they were no longer satisfied to live in caves or belly-high brush shelters made from a few twigs. They began to build round pit houses which were for the most part underground—dug into the earth with a circle of posts supporting a roof of branches covered with mud. Most of these structures had an entrance tunnel and a fire pit in the center of the floor. The tunnel also served as a ventilation shaft sucking up fresh air from the outside while the warm smoke from the fire escaped through a hole in the roof. These pit houses were a great improvement, warm in the winter and cool in the summer.

It is possible that these dwellings, more than half submerged in the soil, are the earliest ancestors of the modern kivas—the ceremonial underground chambers of today's Pueblo Indians.

While the pit house seems to have originated in the Southwest,

Brush shelters such as this, jokingly called "squaw-coolers," were probably erected by the Southwest's earliest inhabitants. They are still used by Indians today for outdoor cooking and for relaxing during the hot summer months.

another important invention—the grinding stone—was borrowed from Central America. Even now the *metate* is a typical everyday household appliance in a Mexican or Pueblo village. The *metate* is a rough stone with a flat or hollow surface, on which corn is ground into meal by hand with a smaller stone called a *mano*. Oddly enough *metates* were in use even before the beginnings of corn planting because many of the nuts and roots gathered by the foragers had also to be ground before they could be eaten. But it was with farming that the grinding stone really came into its own. In Canyon de Chelly, Arizona, huge communal grinding stones have been found at which

Since time immemorial the Indians of the Southwest have used the
*metate*—the corn-grinding stone. Even before they began planting corn,
they used it to crush wild nuts and acorns. Grinding corn on a *metate*
is women's work, and hard work it is.

a number of women could work at the same time. Even at the dawn
of history corn grinding was a social affair during which people
gossiped or sang while crushing the kernels between the *metate* and
the *mano*. Nor is there a basic difference between a *metate* made
eight thousand years ago and one made and used today.

In the course of time people learned to weave mats, sandals, nets,
clothing, and baskets out of yucca fibers. More important, they began
to make pots of clay. Pottery, in the Cochise culture, began sometime around 300 B.C. Pots were made by the coil method. Clay was
rolled between the hands into lengths of thin, sausagelike coils and
built up to the desired height and shape. The inside and outside of

the pot were then smoothed with a flat piece of wood or slab of slate. This is still the method employed. The pottery makers of the Southwest never used a potter's wheel.

Pottery came to North America from the much older civilizations of Mexico. Its introduction proves that prehistoric peoples were not isolated from one another, but that cultural skills were transmitted from region to region and from tribe to tribe.

Much of early Southwestern pottery resembles basketry as a mat of plant fiber is pressed into the clay's surface to make a "woven" pattern. From this fact some writers have reasoned that pottery was discovered spontaneously. Perhaps some woman, on a sudden inspiration, smeared the outside of her baskets with clay to make them watertight. At a later date she left such a basket by accident near a cooking fire and found the clay hardened by the heat. It might have happened this way, at some time or place throughout the ages, but probably not to the Cochise people. They gained their knowledge of pottery making from their southern neighbors. It is evidence of the great respect for old things as well as old people, among New Mexico and Arizona Indians, that the "woven," basket-surfaced pottery, the so-called corrugated ware, was made for hundreds of years, long after its makers had forgotten how the pattern came into existence.

Pottery was another milestone in the life of the people. Corn and seeds stored in clay jars were almost imperishable and could be used for food years after they had been cached. Carrying and storing water was also made easier, even though the prehistoric Indians had learned to make fine, tightly woven baskets in which liquid could be kept for some length of time. And, of course, clay pots brought about a revolution in cooking.

Planting their crops, their storage jars overflowing with maize, secure and snug in their pit houses, these early Americans had become masters of their environment while living in harmony with it. Across the abyss of time we hail them as our first farmers who handed on their achievements to those who came after them. These inheritors were the people of the Mogollon culture, named after mountains in Southeast Arizona and New Mexico because sites of this cultural group were first unearthed there and in adjacent areas reaching from the Upper Gila River to the Rio Grande. It is hard to say where Cochise culture ends and Mogollon begins. Some experts say that the Mogollon people are simply the earlier Cochise people after they became better farmers and potters. The Mogollon way of life continued from about 200 B.C. to A.D. 1100—by and large unaltered except for changing pottery styles.

The Mogollon culture, which in its latest stages coincided with the Pueblos who build their famous cities beneath the overhanging cliffs of Mesa Verde, was distinguished by its own special features.

Pottery shards are the archaeologist's friends. Their form, color, and design tell the expert which people were at what place at what time.

The Mogollon introduced the bow and arrow into the Southwest, and those tribes that still had only spears and *atlatls* must have looked upon them with awe. The Mogollon built pit houses very much like their predecessors, but the house in the center of their villages was always much bigger than the ones that surrounded it. It was probably a communal and religious center. The Mogollon gambled and played games. They bent their dead into a tight, fetal position before burying them in shallow pits.

Their pottery was at first unpainted and later decorated with red designs on a brown background. At the end of their era, they borrowed the designs of their cliff-dwelling northern neighbors. They made stemmed and sawtoothed spear and arrow points. They also made pipes of stone to smoke their native tobacco, probably a mixture of bark and various herbs. The solemnly smoked stone pipe has always been sacred to all Native Americans. Could the belief in the sacred pipe have started here, in the extreme Southwest? We can only speculate.

The Mogollon might have been the first to domesticate the dog and the wild turkey. These two animals were the only ones kept by Indians before the arrival of the white man. Such beasts as are kept today by the herdsmen of the Southwest—horses, burros, cattle, sheep, pigs, and goats—were introduced by the Spaniards. The Indian gave such valuable gifts to the Old World as corn, tobacco, beans, squash, rubber, and chocolate—first drunk by Hernando Cortez at the court of the Mexican emperor Montezuma. One writer has remarked, tongue in cheek, that the Indian did not domesticate the turkey, the turkey domesticated the Indian. Like the western jay who will steal the bacon from a camper's frying pan, the turkey was a bird that could not be kept away from humans. Attracted to the ancient settlements like pigeons to a statue, the only way to cope with it was to coop it up in a cage and give it the status of a domesticated fowl. Similarly, the dog might have sought out man,

Bow and arrows must have seemed a terrible new wonder-weapon to tribes having only spears and *atlatls* to defend themselves. It took primitive hunters centuries to invent and develop the bow, which was effective at over twice the distance of the earlier *atlatl*-propelled dart.

rather than the other way around, from the moment when the first orphaned wolf or coyote puppy snuggled up to a human being for comfort, warmth, and food.

The Mogollon people, in turn, gave way to the Hohokam, a Pima word meaning "those who have gone." The Hohokam have also been called the "Desert Tamers" and the "World's First Etchers." Across a gulf of centuries the Hohokam speak to us through their works of art and their many achievements that leave us charmed and a little mystified. The Hohokams' world was southern Arizona in the Phoenix and Casa Grande areas. The center of their world was Skoaquik, or Snaketown, some thirty miles south of Phoenix, which was rediscovered in 1927. Around it, stretching in every direction, many other Hohokam sites have been found. Close to two hundred houses were excavated at Snaketown showing that here was a good-size population center covering an area of three hundred acres. Even more remarkable, Snaketown was occupied by the same people for over a thousand years without any traces of war and violence.

The Hohokam thrived from 300 B.C. to A.D. 1400. Their culture reached its highest point about A.D. 1000. They live on today in their descendants—the Pima. Again and again we are struck by this enchanting sense of timelessness in this land of sun, silence, and adobe.

The prehistoric peoples of North America left no written records. We must piece together, bit by bit, their history and way of life from the fragments dug up at the sites they occupied. We thus get glimpses of the Hohokam which show us that they had a great sense of order and cooperation, as well as beauty and humor, still characteristics of Indian village dwellers today. Looking at their artifacts and the remains of their settlements like a detective looking at clues, "peeling back the centuries," as Emil W. Haury, the Hohokam's chief interpreter, has called it, we can guess much. We can see that they borrowed from the great cultures far to the south. In fact, nowhere else in North America is this borrowing from the ancient Mexican civilizations so obvious and convincing as among the Hohokam. But while they adopted ball courts and, in a very rudimentary way, the temple pyramid from the far-away southern empires of the Mayas and Aztecs, they did not import their hierarchies and class distinctions. Unlike them, the Hohokam were a peaceful, democratic people. Their houses were all alike, none better than the other, by which we know that they were not divided into castes of nobles and laborers. The Hohokam built no palaces and therefore had no kings.

Their dwellings were structures of cottonwood and mesquite beams, sunk a foot into the ground, covered with mattings and mud. They were much like the Pima houses of today. Those who study them often wonder why the talented Hohokam never advanced beyond these simple, wattled dwellings. But this is putting our values on the gentle Hohokam who cannot answer back. Perhaps if they could they would point out that they had no need for more imposing structures. They lived in a desert climate, they did not have to "keep up with the Joneses." They did not have to build fortified houses of stone because they had no enemies. They built houses that exactly met their needs. If these could be put up in a day or two, so much the better. It enabled them to put their efforts and imagination to work in other fields. The Hohokam may also have used brush shelters for outdoor cooking during the hot summer months. So do many Indian people today. These simple structures—essentially four poles with a roof of branches—are humorously called "squaw-coolers." They are a great comfort for the desert housewife and, as someone has pointed out, need no air conditioning.

The Hohokams' greatest achievements were their irrigation canals, which eventually became huge networks stretching over 150 miles. Diverting river water to "give drink to the thirsty fields," this irrigation network was started as early as 300 B.C. Only people willing to work together for the good of all could have conceived such an enterprise and maintained it over hundreds of years with no machines but only the labor of their hands. The Hohokam tended every square foot of their fields with loving care. They knew their land as they knew their own bodies and treated it accordingly.

The Hohokam liked to beautify themselves. With life so well regulated and with a secure food supply, the diligent farmers had

Seashell ornaments, some in the form of toads, adorned the ancient Hohokam. Similar ornaments are still made by the Zuñi people today.

the luxury of leisure time. Among their artifacts are many paint boxes made of slate or stone, sometimes in the form of a lizard or horned toad. They are reminiscent of the cosmetic palettes ancient Egyptian ladies used for mixing kohl and other pigments for their eye make-up. Hohokam men, as well as women, used their palettes for face and body painting. Paint boxes were often put into graves so that the spirits of the departed could beautify themselves.

The Hohokam also adorned themselves with necklaces, bracelets and earrings. In this respect, too, they showed their inventiveness and refinement by producing deep-etched shell ornaments. A design was outlined on a shell and covered with acid-resisting pitch or resin. The shell was then dropped into a jar of acid made from fermented cactus juice. The acid ate away that part of the surface not covered by the resin, and the figure of, say, a lizard was etched out. The Hohokam perfected this process around A.D. 1100—centuries before European artisans used a similar process to etch ornaments into body armor, shields, and helmets. The possession of shell ornaments indicates that the Hohokam traded far and wide, because the shells had to come from the Pacific Coast over three hundred miles away. Modern Zuñi jewelers still make similar shell

ornaments—not etched but inlaid with turquoise, jet, and coral—
thus carrying on an ancient tradition.

At a late stage in their development the Hohokam raised cotton.
They were skilled weavers, not satisfied with manufacturing simple
cloth but also making twill, gauze, and a lacy, netlike openwork
pattern of decorative weaving. A few copper bells were found at
Hohokam sites. These, too, were imports from abroad, possibly
used as dancing bells. If so, it would again point to the agelessness of
Indian customs, because modern Native Americans also use ankle
bells in their dances, the bells' melodious jingle-jangle being a typical powwow sound effect.

The Hohokam were also imaginative potters. Between the first and
seventh centuries A.D., they made small, whimsical, slit-eyed figurines, possibly for toys but more likely as gifts for the departed. They
made incense burners in the shape of animals and pots in the shape
of human beings—fat, pot-bellied little men covered with geometric
designs. They also made charming, lifelike stone sculptures. Unfortunately they deliberately smashed their beautiful ceramics and
stone figures, "killing them" so that they could serve the dead in
the afterworld. In the same way, modern Pueblo people break a
pottery jar and place the pieces on the grave of a relative.

While their neighbors buried their dead, the Hohokam cremated
them. Cultures, as well as people, die. But in the case of the Hohokam, one should perhaps not speak of dying, but rather of a gentle
half-vanishing. Around A.D. 1100 Snaketown came to its end; it
was abandoned without any sign of war or conquest. The surrounding Hohokam villages seemed to have flourished for another three
hundred years. Around A.D. 1400 occurs an intermingling with the
Anasazi culture to the north—the civilization of the prehistoric
Pueblos. The newcomers were absorbed peacefully. The Hohokam
are the Vanished Ones. Their canals are silted over, and desert winds
blow dust across their settlements. But the Hohokam live on in their

descendants, the Pimas, and also probably in the Pueblos, the sturdy irrigation farms of today. To them, and to the other sedentary corn planters of the Southwest, the Hohokam bequeathed love of peace and a respect for the life-giving corn and for water.

Among some southwestern tribes a man who has killed an enemy, even in self-defense, must purify himself for sixteen days, to cure his spirit of the madness of shedding blood. It sounds like a custom the gentle Hohokam could have started. No culture really dies in the Southwest.

# 4 ▪ THE ANCIENT ONES

*Now bring the Corn, Our Mother,*
*Bring the life-giving Corn*
*In all our thought and words*
*Let us do only good;*
*In all our acts and words*
*Let us be all as one*

PUEBLO MEDICINE SONG

*Anasazi* is a Navajo word. It means "the ancient ones," "the old people." The Navajos gave the name to those who built cities of stone inside the cliffs of Mesa Verde, who built the world's first multistoried apartment houses in Chaco Canyon and elsewhere, and who then mysteriously disappeared leaving the monuments of their culture behind them.

The Anasazi are the ancestors of the modern Pueblo Indians of Arizona and New Mexico, to whom they have passed on a way of life that goes back over a thousand years. The Anasazi's home was the Four Corners area—southeastern Utah, southwestern Colorado, northeastern Arizona, and northwestern New Mexico. "Four Corners" is a white man's expression that is less than a hundred years old. Some of the states to which it refers did not exist until 1912. The area was Mexican until 1848. To the Indians the word has no meaning. "These state border lines are something the white man has drawn up to amuse himself," said one old Hopi. "Why should we pay any attention to them."

This is the Land of Enchantment, as Charles Lummis, who loved it so well, called it, "a land of sun, silence, adobe, and mystery, where the opiate sun soothes to rest, the adobe is made to lean against, and the hush of day-long noon is unbroken."

The Anasazi, during their golden age, were in some ways ahead of many European people living at the same time. While most medieval Europeans slaved as lowly serfs for feudal lords, many Indians of the Southwest lived in apartment houses, wore clothes of fine cotton, practiced the arts of peace, and enjoyed a democratic form of self-rule.

Throughout most of the nineteenth century archaeology was in its infancy. There was no uniform way of naming the various cultures found, and no reliable way of dating them. Every archaeologist had his own pet names and theories. In order to clear up this confusion, the foremost southwestern experts came together in 1927, at Pecos, New Mexico, to agree upon a system of terminology and dating. They divided the Anasazi culture into eight periods spanning two thousand years of human history and came up with the following table:

| | |
|---|---|
| *Basket Makers I* | *Dates unknown* |
| *Basket Makers II* | *Birth of Christ*–A.D. *450* |
| *Basket Makers III* | *450–750* |
| *Pueblo I* | *750–900* |
| *Pueblo II* | *900–1100* |
| *Pueblo III* | *1100–1300* |
| *Pueblo IV* | *1300–1700* |
| *Pueblo V* | *1700–present* |

To understand the Anasazi, we must start with the Basket Makers who came before them. The name Basket Makers is misleading. Basket Makers, simply put, are Anasazi who have not yet learned to make pottery; the Anasazi, in turn, are the early Pueblo Indians, the ancestors of the Hopis, Zuñis, and Taos Indians of today.

At this point the reader might ask, "Why bother about people who have not even learned to make pottery? This is supposed to be a book about Native Americans of today, and here we are still

Pueblo Indians of today are still making baskets the same way the early Basket Makers did. This is Vera Poujouma, a Hopi lady well known for her skill in basket making.

bogged down in pit houses." Maybe Paul S. Martin in his book *Indians Before Columbus* expressed best the reason why we should delve into the eternal yesterday:

And so the value of archaeology lies in developing a new way of looking at life, in searching for truth and beauty where it leads us, and in helping us to understand our times and problems . . . perhaps if all of us put our heads together we can discover the causes for the rise and decline of civilizations and perhaps save our own from disappearing.

Understanding the Ancient Ones is particularly important in the Southwest where, as an early writer put it, "certain old instincts run in all blood," and where people today still grind corn on *metates* and carry babies around in cradle boards as the Anasazis did centuries ago.

The Basket Makers were given that name by Richard Wetherill, a cattle rancher turned archaeologist who discovered many famous southwestern sites, including what is now Mesa Verde National Park. Pueblo Indians, of course, would laugh at the notion that their ancestors were "discovered." They had known about the Old Ones all the time.

Wetherill and many of his contemporaries started out as simple pot hunters, systematically stripping ancient ruins of artifacts, which they often sold to rich collectors. They were no worse than most nineteenth-century archaeologists, such as Heinrich Schliemann who excavated the "Ancient Troy" of Homer's *Iliad*. To them archaeology was mainly a treasure hunt, and they themselves were nothing more than glorified grave-robbers. In 1893 Wetherill found ninety mummified bodies in a Utah cave together with a great number of finely woven baskets. He therefore called the people who made them Basket Makers.

The Basket Makers represent an in-between stage from the oldest desert cultures to the Anasazi. Arriving in the Four Corners area some two thousand years ago, they drifted there in small bands. We must admire them. Without sharp metal, pottery, cotton, beasts of burden, or bow and arrow, they relied on their knowledge of nature. Using only wood, bone, stone, yucca fibers, cedar bast, their own hair spun into cords, and darts propelled by the *atlatl*, they managed to provide everything they needed for their simple life.

At the turn of the century some writers referred to the Basket Makers as "the Mummy People" because so many of their bodies were found in a well-preserved state with the skin, flesh, and hair intact. One could even make out the features of some individual faces. But it is wrong to call these long dead Basket Makers mummies. A real mummy, as found in an ancient Egyptian grave, represents an effort to preserve the body artificially through embalming. No such effort was made by the Basket Makers. Their dead simply turned into "natural mummies" who were preserved by the dry climate.

Why are archaeologists always so excited when they find a southwestern "mummy"? Not for a ghoulish thrill. The physical examination of the bodies can yield much important information. It told the scientists that the Basket Makers were a handsome people, somewhat stocky and smaller than today's Indians. It told them much about their health. Many sicknesses of the Ancient Ones were diagnosed, from bladder stones to arthritis. Their diseases gave valuable hints about their struggle for life. Their teeth were often worn down by the corn they ate—mixed as it was with grit from their *metates*. Poor teeth resulted also from continuously flattening plant fibers between the teeth while making baskets. In a similar way, modern Plains Indians work their teeth down to stumps by flattening porcupine quills between them while decorating a fine war shirt with quillwork designs.

We can learn what kind of food the ancient people ate. More important, a study of bodies over a thousand years old can tell us much about the people who buried them. Among the bodies are those of very old and crippled people who for years must have been unable to fend for themselves. They could have survived only if they were cared for by their families or community. Thus we know that the Anasazi were a compassionate people who respected their elders, and did not abandon them. This same respect for old age we find among today's Pueblos.

The dead were often buried in slab-lined storage cisterns, usually in a fetal position. They were given valuables to take with them to another world—an *atlatl* and spear, clothing, pottery, baskets, and food. They were wrapped in mats, feather blankets, or animal skins, and their heads were covered with a basket. This tells us that the Anasazi believed in an afterlife, and that they thought the spirits of their dead could make use of many things in another world. The dead were also given a new pair of sandals to make their last journey comfortable. Modern Plains Indians also make special burial moc-

Here early Pueblo culture is pictured in a nutshell—or rather in a pottery bowl, put into a grave as a gift to the departed spirit for use in another world. The bowl contained two small ears of corn, a bone dagger, a hairbrush of yucca leaves, a weasel skin (which may have been a medicine charm), a woven pouch full of seeds, a shell necklace, and a turquoise pendant.

casins for their dead, with fully beaded soles for the long road along the Milky Way to the Spirit Land. Did the southwestern Indians of long ago influence their northern neighbors of the plains? Our knowledge of the material culture of prehistoric people comes to us, in large measure, from things found in their graves. In one Anasazi burial site no less than six hundred different articles were found beside the body of a man. He must have been a highly respected person. His relatives gave him everything he might need in another world—every imaginable tool, weapon, household appliance, or food used by his people at the time of his death. In a few cases even dogs were slain and put in the grave to follow their masters to the Spirit World.

We also learn a little history from the graves. In the Canyon Del Muerto archaeologists came upon a massacre site—Basket Makers slain by enemies with a new and terrible weapon: the bow. One of the bodies had an arrowhead sticking between the ribs. The poor Basket Makers had only their darts and *atlatls,* but the peaceful farmers defended themselves to the last. Such direct evidences of battle are rare. Generation followed generation without signs of war and violence—much different from our own time.

Finally, digging up a grave can confront us with mystery. What are we to think of a corpse cut in half, then sewn together again? Or what can we make of the puzzle of two buried hands? Or of two Basket Maker's arms cut off at the elbows, the hands resting palms upward on a base of grass, which were found in the Canyon Del Muerto. The grave was untouched, yet there was no trace of the missing body. The grave with the two hands contained gifts—a new pair of sandals, three necklaces, and a large stone pipe. No wonder the wife of the archaeologist who unearthed it, Ann Axtell Morris, was mystified. She wrote about "shoes without feet, necklaces without a neck, and a pipe without a mouth." Some speculate that a man may have been killed by a rockfall with only his hands sticking out of the rubble. These had been cut off to be buried properly. Or maybe a man had been mangled by a bear or mountain lion who had left nothing behind but the victim's arms. Was this the answer? We may never know.

Archaeologists and anthropologists look upon the digging up of prehistoric graves as a necessary part of their work, but more and more Indians view these activities with deep misgivings. "How would you white people feel about it if we Indians dug up your ancestors' graves and put the remains of your grandparents in museum cases for everybody to stare at?" AIM, the militant American Indian

Many modern Indians do not like the digging up of old Indian graves and the exhibition of human remains in museum displays. "How would you like us digging up your ancestors," they say, "putting their bones in a glass case for all to see?"

Movement, is in the forefront of this fight. AIM members have entered museums and forcibly removed prehistoric human remains for reburial. In some localities where scientists were excavating Native American graves, activist Indians began digging up grave-stones of whites to put on exhibit. Indians of the Southwest feel insulted by a display of a female mummy at Mesa Verde National Park, playfully known as "Esther" to white visitors. Many also are opposed to medicine bundles and sacred objects being on display in museums. "These holy things should not be stared at, or fingered by curious tourists," is the way many young Native Americans voice their resentment.

There are, as the table shows, the periods Basket Makers I, Basket Makers II, and Basket Makers III. Basket Makers I exist, so far, only in archaeologists' minds. No trace of them has been found.

This Papago dwelling, photographed in 1894, is made of wattle—of sticks put fairly close together with the spaces between them filled with hardened mud and stones. A few similar structures can still be found in Papago and in villages in Arizona. At an early stage the Anasazi used similar methods to build their homes.

Because Basket Makers II had reached a comparatively high stage of human development, the experts reason that Basket Makers I came before them, men who, as yet, did not know how to plant corn. The experts certainly have logic on their side, but Basket Makers I have thus far remained in hiding.

Basket Makers II emerge at the beginning of the Christian era. They were marginal farmers, who still depended to a certain extent on hunting and the gathering of wild plants. At first, they had no bows, no pottery, no cotton, no beans, and no turkeys. But they started, as one writer said, "the long upward climb, the molding of a new way of life, a thousand years in the making."

With their digging sticks they knew how to plant a tropical, small-eared variety of corn. They stored the corn and squash in slab-walled cists and jar-shaped holes. Besides corn, they ate pine nuts, sunflower seeds, roots, and certain varieties of cactus. They also ate rabbits, gophers, and field mice. They were very inventive hunters. A net 240 feet long has been found in one of their sites. Made of more than four miles of string, it was probably spread across a narrow gulch while a whole tribe beat the bushes, shouting and waving their arms, driving all the rabbits thereabouts into the net. It even had a dark spot in the middle to mislead the rabbits into taking it for a hole through which they could escape. Working together in this way, a band could catch much more game than individual hunters could.

The Basket Makers built domed, saucer-shaped houses of sticks smeared with mud. At a later stage of development these were not pit houses but entirely above ground. The floor of these dwellings was often plastered over with clay or covered with stone slabs. At one point in their development the smokehole of their houses became a hatchway which people used to go in and out by means of a ladder. This set a pattern for fifteen hundred years. Many modern Pueblo kivas are still entered this way, from the top, as are the traditional houses, many of which are still lived in.

Once the hatchway and ladder system was introduced, the entrance tunnel of the pit dwellings was kept as a mere ventilation shaft. Many of the Basket Makers' houses had a shallow hole in the center of the floor which very probably represented *Sipapu,* the place of emergence, through which spirits could enter a household. This shows that the religious beliefs of modern Pueblos go back to the beginnings of Anasazi culture. "With us," said an old Hopi lady, "things change slowly, if at all. . . . We cling to our old ways, and the highway, out there, and the electric towers over the horizon, and all the tourists, these things cannot change our hearts."

Living in a sunny climate, the Basket Makers had no use for a wardrobe. In summer a simple loincloth or string apron was all they needed. Their most important item of clothing was a pair of sturdy, thick-soled sandals made of plant fibers. Anyone who has ever trudged through the chaparral, the cactus- and thorn-strewn southwestern landscape, will appreciate this. During the winter people wrapped themselves in blankets made of strings, around which pieces of rabbit fur were twined. The strings were tied together to make a strong yet light covering.

Though not fancy dressers, the Basket Makers spent much time on their appearance. They gave their dead relatives hairbrushes made from bundles of stiff yucca leaves so that they could keep themselves neat in the afterworld. Males often had very elaborate hairdos; Women's hair, on the other hand, was cut short in the fashion of today's Pueblo women. Do Pueblo women wear their hair short because once, in the dim past, their ancestresses had cut theirs off to twist it into ropes and string, and the fashion, once started, lasted to this day?

The Basket Makers loved ornaments. They wore necklaces, bracelets, and ear pendants made of bone, stone, and especially shell. Did modern Pueblo women, bedecking themselves on fiesta days, inherit their love of jewelry from these ancient ancestors?

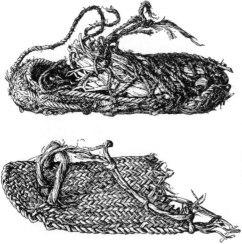

Sandals woven from plant fibers were typical among the Basket Makers as well as the Anasazi.

The people were fond of music, which played a big role in their religious ceremonies. They made rattles of deer hooves and bones to be used in their rituals. They made bird-bone whistles similar to those made from an eagle's wing bone, which are used today during the Sun Dance of the Plains Indians. They had flutes. In one grave were four beautifully made flutes. Did the Basket Makers already have a Flute Clan, as some modern pueblos do? Was the dead man its priest? Or was he simply a master flute player? We will never know. One thing we do know is that the figure of Kokopilli, the legendary hump-backed flute player, became a frequent design-motif of the Ancient Ones, painted over and over on pottery bowls and canyon walls.

But pottery came later. The early Anasazi are not called Basket Makers for nothing. They made baskets of every kind: carrying baskets that fit the shoulders like modern backpacks, trays, bowls, tightly woven and pitch-lined water bottles, baskets with narrow openings for storing seeds or other small objects. Baskets were even used for cooking. By pouring water into a basket and then dropping one or two heated stones into it, one could obtain a hot soup. Often baskets were decorated with handsome black geometric designs. The Basket Makers also discovered that a person's head is better fitted to carry burdens than any other part of the body. They made head straps of plant fibers which went around the forehead and were then tied to a burden carried on the back. Leaning forward, it was then easy to carry even a large and heavy load.

The Basket Makers' religious beliefs must have been similar to those held by many modern Indians. Corncobs decorated with feathers are not unlike prayer offerings made by today's Pueblos. The Basket Makers had medicine bundles and pipes which are sacred to Native Americans in our time. The Basket Makers had the custom of tying a baby's umbilical cord to his cradle. Just so do Sioux and Blackfeet Indians of today sew up their babies' navel cords in beaded turtle and lizard-shaped bags which they tie to their cradle boards as good-luck charms. Again we find that among Native Americans certain beliefs and customs seem to endure.

Around A.D. 450, Basket Makers II, without being the least aware of it, and by the decision of people living fifteen hundred years later, became Basket Makers III, or Modified Basket Makers. *Modified,* in archaeological language, means "improved." These Modified Basket Makers had learned better methods of farming and irrigation. Besides corn and squash they acquired an important new crop: beans! Dependent mainly on planting, they could spend less time moving about in search of wild food. They settled down in permanent settlements, becoming, as the archaeologists say, "sedentary." Family groups and small bands joined together in villages. These often consisted of two rows of houses joined together in an arc somewhat like a subway train traveling in a shallow curve.

The Modified Basket Makers had three things their predecessors had to do without: pottery, the turkey, and the bow. At first, pottery was crude, made of gray, sun-dried unfired mud, often shaped in a basket which served as a mold. It did not take long before pots were fired and decorated. The Basket Makers probably borrowed the art of pottery from their southern neighbors, the Mogollon.

Having the turkey as a second domestic animal was also a big step forward. Turkey meat was tasty, but turkey feathers were more important to the Indians. There were periods during the long history of the Anasazi when turkey meat was taboo and the birds were kept only for their feathers. The soft, downy feathers were split down the middle and wound around fiber strings. These were then tied together to be used as blankets and wraparounds. Feathercloth became a specialty of the Anasazi; it was warm, light, and water-repellent.

The introduction of the bow brought about one of the greatest changes in the Basket Makers' lives. It, too, came to them from their southern neighbors and reached them at a fairly late stage of their development—long after other tribes had acquired it. With the bow came other tools, such as arrow-shaft straighteners. The bow was as superior to the *atlatl*-propelled dart as later the gun would be to the bow. With bow and arrow a hunter could bring down his game at two or three times the distance as with his spear and rabbit stick. One-sided massacres, such as happened in Canyon del Muerto, were a thing of the past. It must have been a tremendous thrill for the hunter to feel this new weapon in his hand, to aim at a stag or mountain lion, sighting along the arrow shaft, to hear the twang of the bowstring.

The Basket Makers III began to decorate the cliffs around them with figures of square-shouldered human beings and the outlines of hands. This was the beginning of rock art which occurred in the form of pictographs and petroglyphs. A pictograph is a design on a cliff painted in color. A petroglyph is a similar design, but it is not painted; it is scratched or chiseled into the rock. Over the centuries Anasazis left their designs on the rock walls—geometric shapes; zig-zags, and wavy lines representing water; whorls, spirals, and circles representing the sun. They depicted people, animals, hunters with bows and arrows, hump-backed flute-players whose feet often seemed to point the wrong way. In Chaco Canyon, New Mexico, one can see, chiseled into the rock, a row of six-toed footprints marching up a cliff.

These rock paintings were not meant as art. Drawing the figure of an antelope gave a man power over the animal. Painting the symbols for sun and water on a rockface was much like praying for the corn to ripen and the rain to fall. Basket Makers III also made clay figurines of women which had religious significance. These small armless and legless images bear a striking resemblance to clay figures of the Mother Goddess found in the Near East and the Mediterranean region. Maybe the ones fashioned by the Basket Makers also repre-

(1) The canyon walls of the Southwest are covered with petroglyphs and pictographs. This is an ancient pictograph. The
human figures are simply painted on the wall in earth colors.
Petroglyphs, like the antelope below, are designs chipped or
pecked out of the stone surface.

(2) Designs, such as these antelope, were probably a sort of hunting magic.
By making an image of the animal, a hunter acquired power over it.

(3) In this petroglyph we see hunters aiming their bows at a huge bear. The exaggerated size of the bear emphasizes the danger and the achievement of killing it.

(4) Could these be Anasazis with shields and clubs defending their village against nomadic raiders?

(5) The coming of friars on horseback is depicted in this old pictograph in Canyon de Chelly.

sented a goddess, the all-nourishing Earth who makes all living things grow and multiply.

In learning new crafts Basket Makers III did not neglect their older arts. Basketry reached its greatest height. They also made wonterfully woven sashes of dog hair with long fringes, every bit as beautiful as the finest sashes made by the modern Pueblos. They made better stone tools—well-polished, notched axe heads and more sophisticated bone implements. Their black-on-gray and red-on-orange pottery became better. By A.D. 700, Basket Makers III were ready to become Pueblo I.

*Pueblo* is a Spanish word. It can mean a number of things: a people, a tribe, a village, a town. Here it is used as a name for a cultural period, the various later Anasazi periods Pueblo I, II, and III. The Anasazis are the direct ancestors of the modern Pueblo Indians, the settled, corn-growing, city-building farmers of Arizona and New Mexico who are all inheritors of a common culture.

At first, the people designated Pueblo I were thought to be a different race from the Basket Makers. The Basket Makers had narrow, elongated skulls, the Pueblo I people had round-shaped heads.

For a number of years, archaeologists wrote about new tribes of round-headed invaders driving away the long-headed Basket Makers, but in the end they found out that the "round skulls" and the "long skulls" were one and the same people. The new head shape was the result of a new kind of cradle board adopted by the Anasazi. The Basket Makers' cradle had been soft, pliant, and padded. The new cradle consisted of wooden boards against which the baby's head was strapped. This flattened the backs of still soft skulls. The result was the "round head" of the "new" race. A number of Indian tribes using wooden cradle boards have produced "flat-headed" people. They probably found the artificially flattened head handsome.

Young Pueblo children often have the back of their heads straight and flattened, supposedly the result of spending their first months strapped in a wooden cradle board. Cradle boards were already used by the early Anasazi.

The Pueblo I and II periods, which lasted from 700 to 1100, are known as Development Pueblo, "development" being another frequent term to denote the beginning stage of a new cultural epoch. There was really no sharp dividing line between the Basket Makers and the Pueblo. The population increased. Villages became larger and more numerous, spreading out from the Four Corners area.

During Development Pueblo the Anasazi became skillful builders. Most houses were no longer made of poles and sticks, but of stones imbedded in adobe. Later, people shaped sandstone with hammers made of harder rock into building stones fitted so well that they needed little or no mortar to hold them together. Houses were so strongly constructed that they could support a second or third floor. The dwellings were entered by means of ladders through openings in the flat roofs. There were no doors, a defensive precaution. In case of a raid by nomadic tribes, the Anasazis had only to draw up the ladders to make their homes into fortresses; but little evidence has been found of any warlike happenings. Maybe the Anasazi were overcautious. As was true during the Basket Maker III period, vil-

Kivas are as old as the Pueblos themselves. There was usually a kiva for every religious society. The many kivas of Pueblo Bonito, New Mexico, prove that this huge 12th-century city had many of these societies.

An above-ground kiva at Namke. A kiva is a Pueblo's spiritual and religious center. Some Pueblos have many kivas; a few have none left. A kiva is a place in which young boys are taught the traditions and legends of their people.

lages were made up of connected "unit houses" inhabited by people related through a common grandmother or great-grandmother.

Each village contained a number of the characteristic kivas. We have heard this word before and will hear it again, because the kiva has always played an enormous role in the life of the Pueblo Indians. The kivas of the Anasazi were in their main features identical with those in use today.

The typical kiva was round, made of stones, its roof flush with the ground. Some modern kivas, at Santo Domingo, for instance, while still circular are built above ground. Steps or ladders lead up to a roof with an opening in the center from which it is entered. Some kivas, such as in Acoma, are square rooms on the ground floor of ancient houses. Modern kivas thus represent all the prehistoric building styles. In ancient times a kiva always contained a fire pit with a deflector—an upright slab of stone—which prevented the air that came through the ventilation shaft from blowing out the fire. Each kiva also contained a *Sipapu,* a hole through which the Kachinas, supernatural beings, could emerge during a religious ceremony. Unless such a ritual was in progress the *Sipapu* was covered up so that no spirits would enter at the wrong time. All around the inside of a kiva ran a bench which people could use for sitting down or as a shelf. Poles or columns held up the roof.

Kivas, especially during a ceremony, might contain altars, sand paintings, and sacred objects. Dancers assembled in a kiva to emerge in the guise of gods to act out a holy legend. Kivas were a place for learning. In them old men taught young boys the prayers and songs of their people. When nearing adulthood, boys might spend long periods of time inside the underground chambers preparing themselves to become men. Kivas were also used as clubhouses where men came together to chat and set up a weaving loom. Weaving was a man's job. The fact that kivas were places for men only does not mean that women were discriminated against. On the contrary, women played a main role in the life of the Anasazi—then and now. Men traced their descent through their mothers. They belonged to their mothers' clan and entered its kiva where they were taught not by their fathers, who belonged to a different kiva, but by their uncles on the mother's side. Men lived in their wives' village and in their wives' houses. Women were the property owners. It is still so among modern Pueblos.

Men and women performed the different tasks tradition had assigned to them. Women did all the pottery, men all the weaving. Women built the homes, though the men carried the heavy wooden beams. Men did the hunting, women made the baskets. In this division of labor it fell to the men to hand on the people's religious beliefs to future generations and to be in charge of the sacred rituals. For this reason the kivas became a man's world.

There were as many kivas in a village as there were clans and religious societies. One famous Anasazi cliff town contained twenty-three kivas for an estimated population of three hundred. Now and then a clan died out. Then its kiva stood empty and mute, the sound of drums and rattles which had once filled it only a memory. Kivas are still abandoned as old traditions are given up by some of today's Pueblos. It is a sad thing, but nothing new. Certain rituals and prayers were jealously guarded and kept secret from all but the members of one specific kiva. The kivas are believed patterned after the pit houses, the earliest Anasazi dwellings, and they continued to be built that way after pit houses were replaced by above-ground stone or adobe houses. This has been cited as an indication of the Pueblos' stubborn adherence to tradition, but some of this "reaching back" is common to all mankind. In modern America one can see churches built like medieval cathedrals with pointed spires, stained-glass windows, and gargoyles. Finally, it should be mentioned that in the older books kivas are often called *estufas,* the Spanish word for "stove." It is a word that has lately gone out of fashion.

Before the Development Pueblo period, the Anasazi had borrowed much from the Mogollon culture in the south. Now this progress began to reverse itself. It was now the Mogollons' turn to be influenced by the Anasazi, a sign that the Four Corners people were surpassing their southern neighbors in many cultural achievements.

Pottery became ever more beautiful and varied. The art of basketry declined; it was no longer essential. The people often buried their dead under the trash heaps outside their homes. No disrespect was meant by this. They wanted the spirits of their loved ones nearby, and they made the graves where the digging was easy. Animal lovers will like one touching custom: while dead humans were given dogs and turkeys to accompany them to another world, dogs and turkeys in turn sometimes got *their* burial gifts—bones and a few kernels of corn.

The period saw a burst of building activity. People experimented with different types of houses. Pit houses and surface dwellings existed side by side. Houses came in all kinds of shapes. Slabs, adobe bricks, wattle and daub, and stone masonry were some of the materials and methods used, sometimes in combination. Thus the Development Pueblo people set the stage for the fabulous apartment-house builders of Pueblo III, the great or classic Pueblo, the golden age of the Anasazi.

# 5 ▪ CITIES OF MYSTERY

*How many White Americans would*
*Walk four miles to the stone quarry,*
*Quarry stones to make millions of building blocks,*
*Shape all the stones so as to present a smooth face,*
*Do all work with stone malls and hammers,*
*Carry all on one's back to the building site,*
*Cut the timbers with a stone axe, and carry them many miles.*
*(We'd probably live in a tent!)*

NATIONAL MONUMENT PAMPHLET

In an isolated corner of New Mexico, surrounded on all sides by an endlessly stretching desert, lies the magnificent ruin of a town built in the shape of a half moon. We call this ruin by its Spanish name: *Pueblo Bonito*—the Beautiful City. We do not know what the people who lived there called it because they disappeared long ago. For eight hundred years Pueblo Bonito slumbered like a lifeless ghost, half-buried in dust, disturbed by no sound except the rustling of the wind, the cry of a mountain lion, or the scurrying of a lizard over crumbling walls. Even now, it is accessible only by a long ride over lonely, dusty roads where the experienced traveler is distinguished by a waterbag dangling from the car radiator and a spare can of gasoline in his trunk.

Pueblo Bonito is part of Chaco Canyon National Monument, which has many ruins. For hundreds of years wandering Navajos had known the place but had kept away from this abode of the Chindees, the spirits of the dead who could bring a man nothing but bad luck. In 1910 Richard Wetherill, the discoverer of so many ancient sites, and one of the first white men to explore Pueblo Bonito, was shot dead while riding with one of his hired hands through Chaco Canyon. "There you are," said the Navajos. "Those

Pueblo Bonito, New Mexico, taken from the high cliffs rising behind the ancient ruins. Built between A.D. 1050 and 1130, this city was one huge semicircular complex of 800 connected units housing some 1,200 inhabitants; the world's first "apartment house."

Anasazi do not like anyone to dig up their bones." The excavation of Pueblo Bonito was finally accomplished by the National Geographic Society in the years 1921 to 1927.

Pueblo Bonito is not a city of individual dwellings, but one huge apartment house of some eight hundred rooms. The first modern six-story apartment house, by comparison, was not built until 1896 —in New York. Pueblo Bonito has been likened to the famous Habitad of Expo 67 at the Montreal World's Fair.

Into its construction went over 50 million pieces of stone, quarried, transported, chipped into shape, and laid in rows. Built between 1050 and 1130, it was for a while the center of Anasazi culture. At Pueblo Bonito, the great age of the Anasazi had its beginning.

Even as an empty ruin, Pueblo Bonito exerts its magic on the visitor. Defying the batterings of centuries, it stands in silent grandeur. From a cliff rising behind the Pueblo, one has a bird's eye

An early imaginary reconstruction of an apartment-house-type Anasazi Pueblo built like a fortress for defense.

view of the gigantic D-shaped ruin with its many kivas, but it looks even more impressive as you get closer. Its builders had the knack of packing the greatest number of tenants into the smallest possible space. The masonry is pleasing to the eye, the finest of any found among prehistoric sites in North America. The walls consist of alternating rows of small and larger stones, which rise into beautiful banded patterns. The stones are fitted together so well that it is often impossible to insert a knife blade between them. There are long vistas of doorways. Many doors are keyhole-shaped, not only in Pueblo Bonito, but also in other Anasazi ruins. Archaeologists say they do not know why the Ancient Ones built their doors this way. I would like to venture a guess. They were T-shaped to fit a woman carrying a large jar or other burden on her head, as Pueblo women do to this day.

The ancient builders also showed a fine sense of design in the construction of their ceilings, which were made of large crossbeams and small, peeled willow-stick coverings put together in a herring-bone pattern. White architects have adopted this eye-pleasing style of ceiling for modern adobe houses in Santa Fe and Albuquerque. Another outstanding feature in Chaco Canyon are the "great kivas" —enormous subterranean ceremonial chambers more than sixty feet across. These huge structures could accommodate hundreds of worshipers. By way of an underground passage, masked priests could enter the kivas without being seen, to appear mysteriously from the underworld before an awe-struck audience.

Pueblo Bonito, in its heyday, bustled with life. There was a steady coming and going, up and down ladders, with the women deftly balancing large water jars on their heads, some with an additional load—a baby strapped into a cradle board slung over their backs.

The many kiva roofs formed tiny plazas. On them, the women made their pottery, including the city's specialty, a black-on-white mug that much resembles a modern beer stein. Men were busy making hishi-necklaces from strands of turquoise disks, boring holes into each disk by means of a bow drill, very much like the jewelers of Santo Domingo today. One single necklace found in Chaco Canyon contained no less than twenty-five hundred turquoise beads.

Women ground corn on their *metates*. The job was now done in stages. Three grinding stones were set up next to one another, a woman bending over each. The first *metate* was rough and it ground coarse corn. This went to the next *metate* where it was reground. From there, it went to the third and smoothest *metate* to be made into the finest meal. Still, it was never so fine as to be entirely free of grit. An old Pueblo proverb says: "During his life each man must swallow a *metate*." Grinding was hard work. Maybe some men made the women's labor easier by playing their flutes for them as was commonly done in the pueblos of the nineteenth century.

And all the time one could hear the muffled drumbeats from within the kivas, where men rehearsed their songs and dances. In

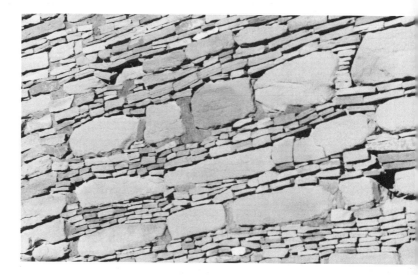

The walls of Pueblo Bonito are made of chipped stones, carefully fitted together so tightly that in places not even a knife blade can be inserted between them. Alternating rows of large and small stones make pleasing patterns, a testament to the Anasazi builders' feeling for design and artistic expression.

the evening the planters came home from their fields with their digging sticks, and the hunters returned with their game. A slain deer was covered with a feather blanket, the hunters kneeling or squatting beside it, asking their prey to forgive them, saying, "We grieve that we had to take your life so that the people might live." As the day came to an end the inhabitants could hear, coming from the highest rooftop, the voice of the town crier telling them to prepare for a ceremonial dance on the next morning. And so the night came.

Pueblo Bonito had its problems. At its back rose an immense cliff. A huge rock weighing more than one hundred thousand tons was on the point of splitting loose from the cliff, threatening to crush part of the town beneath it. Erosion had hollowed out the base of the rock, and the inhabitants worked hard to fill in and brick up the gap. They could have saved themselves the trouble. The big rock came tumbling down with a noise like a thunderclap, wiping out some thirty apartments—*but this was in 1941*, more than eight hundred years after the last inhabitant had left the city.

Another problem for the city dwellers arose when a new tribe moved in with them. Though related, the newcomers were on a different level of development from the original inhabitants; their masonry was immensely superior, and they might even have spoken a different language. They rebuilt one corner of the apartment-house city to their taste, lived there in style, and seemed to have been a little better off than their landlords. Such an accommodation is rare in history and confirms the Anasazi's reputation for being peaceful, good-natured, and adaptable. The two communities occupying the same town may have had their squabbles, but this is only a guess, and a white man's guess at that. Maybe the Anasazi had found the secret that has so long eluded us—how to live in harmony with one's neighbors.

Nomadic raiders seemed to have been a problem, at least in the city dwellers' minds, but excavations show no trace of violence or war. Nevertheless, at one time the townspeople walled up all but one of the entranceways leading into Pueblo Bonito, transforming their apartment house into an impregnable fortress. They probably had good reasons for doing so.

But the real problem was water—or rather, the lack of it. From 1090 to 1101, so the tree rings tell us, the area was in the grip of a terrible drought. The rains ceased to fall and the life-giving stream, on which the fields depended for their irrigation, went dry. In vain the people made beautiful stone and turquoise fetishes in the form of frogs and tadpoles to act as water makers and propitiate the supernaturals. They thought that the drought was a punishment inflicted upon them by the gods. Luck had deserted their city. They left—not all at once, but in a steady trickle. At the height of its prosperity, Chaco Canyon, which contained dozens of sites besides Pueblo Bonito, had sustained a population of some ten thousand people. Soon all were gone. The buildings of the apartment-house city were begun about the year 900. By 1130, it was empty of human life.

An air of mystery surrounds Pueblo Bonito. Only a few bodies of the inhabitants have been found. What happened to the dead? Where were they buried? We do not know. The bones and feathers of fourteen macaws were discovered in the ruins. Macaws are large tropical parrots. How did they get to Pueblo Bonito? Who brought them? Were they kept as sacred birds?

And what happened to those who left the town? Where did they go? The Hopis have a legend that it was their ancestors who built Pueblo Bonito and eventually abandoned it. According to another legend, the snake and flute clans held a sacred race once every year, during which a priest with a large olla full of water was given a big head start while the fastest men tried to catch up with him. The race was a religious ceremony to bring on rain, but in the course of time the people forgot this and ran only for sport. No wonder the Kachina were angry and stopped the rain. Sooner or later, all the cities and cliff dwellings of the Anasazi were abandoned, but not conquered. In some cases, everything was left behind—food, fine pottery, turquoise necklaces. Did the people think that the town and all the goods in it were cursed and that they had to make a completely new start? And was drought the only reason for the exodus? The tree rings say so, but the mystery remains!

In his book *Mesa, Canyon and Pueblo* Charles F. Lummis, who roamed over every mile of this land on foot or on horseback before cars made travel easy, had his own thoughts of why the Ancient Ones deserted their homes:

The savage nomad became too attentive; or drought prevailed; or an epidemic came; or lightning befell the kiva; or any of a thousand other omens indicated the will of the TRUES and forthwith, the Indian changed his town and farm to a new place . . . to befool undreamed-of theorizers.

Everywhere, the great or classic Pueblo period was a time of frenzied building. Near the Animas River, sixty-eight miles north of Pueblo Bonito, in a valley of wild roses, rises Aztec Ruin, the remains of another giant apartment house of the Anasazi. In spite of its name it was not built by the faraway Aztecs of Mexico, but by the refugees from Pueblo Bonito trying to make a new start. This belief rests on the fact that the masonry and pottery are the same in both places.

Aztec was a well-designed and laid-out town. It could be entered only by one gate. It too was a fortress. It also was the home of some two thousand people living in hundreds of connected rooms which rose to a height of three stories at the back of the village. All rooms were grouped around a central plaza with the main kiva in the middle.

It is the Great Kiva which has made Aztec Ruin famous. Forty-eight feet in diameter, and totally rebuilt in all its former grandeur, it is the finest in the United States. It has an inner and an outer ring, the latter made up of fourteen rooms! Possibly the priests lived in them, dressing themselves for a masked dance, keeping some of the rooms for storing sacred objects. Visitors often say that going into the kiva makes them feel like being in a cathedral.

We must feel sorry for the people who so carefully and lovingly built this town, lived in it, and abandoned it all in the space of one short generation. Aztec was started in 1110, and finished fourteen years later. By 1130 it was a sand-swept ghost town, "the stark and glorious memento of a Golden Age."

Again we face a mystery. Why did the inhabitants build their city in such haste only to abandon it with equal speed? Why did

T-shaped entranceway at Aztec ruin, Colorado. This door shape is typical of many prehistoric Pueblo ruins and can still be seen in some of the older Hopi villages.

they wall in all doors and windows, leaving many valuable things in sealed-up rooms? Did they want to preserve them until their return? Did they flee from drought, fire, enemies, or just bad omens?

Between 1225 and 1250, Aztec was once more rebuilt and abandoned. The new builders were not the same people who had lived there before, but another group of Anasazi, possibly from Mesa Verde. They built the new town on the rubble of the old without bothering to unseal the rooms of those who had gone. While the first inhabitants had buried their dead carefully under the floors of their houses together with many grave offerings, the newcomers buried their dead sloppily and in haste, giving them no gifts, as if they could not wait to be rid of them. Had calamity or disease overtaken them? Aztec seems not to have been a happy place to live.

Hundreds of years after the last inhabitants were gone, the ruin was still in for a rough time. White settlers and ranchers coming into the area late in the nineteenth century used it as a quarry to build their own homes. After all, those prehistoric Indians had quarried and dressed the stones better than the settlers could—or would. Why waste all that fine building material? In the same way, Germanic barbarians used carved marble blocks from the noble monuments of ancient Rome to make themselves huts and pigsties.

Later, the splendid ruin became a pot-hunter's paradise. Neighborhood ranchers, storekeepers, cowboys, and schoolchildren spent their weekends ransacking rooms. Soon many homes had a mummy, an odd skull, a few fine pots and artifacts to decorate their living rooms. As tourists became more frequent, one could sell them an old pot as a souvenir, and so the vandalism continued year after year. It was not until 1918 that the ruin was finally protected as a future national monument.

"I'd prefer a gila monster to a pot hunter," said a ranger at Chaco Canyon. Most people would agree with him. Only recently a party of pot hunters was caught by Navajo tribal police and fined. Near Grants, New Mexico, a small truck carrying a load of illegally dug Casa Grande effigy jars overturned and its priceless load was smashed. But the smuggling of prehistoric pottery continues. At $100 to $300 a pot, the unlawful digging is worthwhile.

What is so bad about pot hunting? The individual pot, lost to the public and museums forever, is the least. It is not the loss of the pot that is mourned, but the pot's lost story. Each piece of pottery has something to tell us. An Anasazi jar, for instance, found among the ruins of another culture, might show a relationship between two different people, or at least a trade route. The position of a pot within layers of earth, the objects found with it, might contain a clue to an as yet unsolved mystery. This is why, during an authorized dig, every object found is photographed and sketched in its original position, numbered, and written down in a notebook before its careful removal. A pot or artifact displayed by itself on a curio collector's mantelpiece tells us nothing.

The canyon and mesa lands of the Southwest are dotted with Anasazi ruins, often in places of great scenic beauty. Where else but in the Southwest can one find a place like red-walled Canyon De Chelly—one of America's great natural wonders—which contains many Anasazi ruins, dozens of pictographs and petroglyphs, and which is also the home of modern Navajos who drive their flocks along the sandy canyon bottom. Looking down from the dizzying heights of the canyon's rim, you can see at a glance towering natural erosions, an ancient ruin wedged into the face of the headwall like a swallow's nest (did its inhabitants possess wings?), rock paintings, the tiny figure of a woman working on her loom, and boys racing their ponies among clouds of dust, their thin, high-pitched yells of exultation echoing back four or five times from the purple canyon walls.

Among the Canyon De Chelly sites, White House Ruin, built between 1060 and 1275, is perhaps the best known. It was rendered immortal by such pioneering photographers of the West as William Henry Jackson and Edward S. Curtis who came hundreds of miles on muleback with their ponderous, unhandy cameras, their heavy boxes of wet plates, and very little else.

Almost equally spectacular are the great ruins of Navajo National Monument, near Monument Valley: Keet-Seel and Betatakin. Betatakin is a stunning sight. Situated in an immense natural

White House Ruin, Canyon de Chelly, Arizona, a favorite subject for famous 19th-century photographers.

Betatakin Ruin, Navajo National Monument. This ancient Anasazi settlement is dwarfed by the 400-foot-high cave in which it is situated.

archway four hundred feet high, the ancient village looks tiny, dwarfed, like a handful of children's building blocks. A stiff hike down one canyon wall and part way up the other reveals a good-sized hamlet of 150 rooms, remarkable for having no round kivas. The walk to the ruin and back takes about ninety minutes. It is said that this hike is one mile long going down, and ten miles long coming back up the trail. It certainly seems that way.

At the extreme western limit of the Anasazi's cultural influence, south of Cameron and the Grand Canyon, lies Wupatki, the "Tall House," with its prehistoric ball court. This is a place where civilizations mingle. The buildings look like typical Anasazi dwellings, but the ball court is Hohokam.

Spectacular as all their ruins are, most people know the Anasazi as the cliff dwellers of Mesa Verde, Colorado. On December 18, 1888, Richard Wetherill and his cousin, Charles Mason, were looking for a stray cow. "Charlie, look at that," said Wetherill, pointing to a snow-covered fairy-tale castle with square and round towers nestling into the rock beneath an immense, protective overhang. To his discovery Wetherill gave the name "Cliff Palace." In time it became the best known and most visited Anasazi site. Cliff Palace was something to excite a man—even one like Richard Wetherill, a dour, sober-minded Quaker who neither smoked, drank, nor swore, who spoke very little, and smiled even less.

Cliff Palace became the embodiment of the Ancient Ones. Don Watson, who spent a lifetime studying and writing about Mesa Verde, describes the ruin: "A giant with a shawl of everlasting stone pulled closely about its shoulders, it has stood with unbowed head, an eternal monument to the intelligence and industry of its builders." Of course, Wetherill was as much the discoverer of Cliff Palace as Columbus was of America. Charlie Mason admitted as much, saying that the Utes knew about it and had told the white men about it, only they wouldn't believe them. But they believed their own eyes, and soon the smoke of Wetherhill's campfire rose from one of the old kivas, as the white men camped where once priests had held their sacred rites. It was not hard to keep modern Indians away. As Charlie Mason said, "The Utes were afraid of the ruins because they believed that the spirits of the old people were in them. If we wanted to keep the Utes out of our camp, we just put a skull on a stick and they wouldn't come near."

Later, at Chaco Canyon, Wetherill kept his Navajo diggers on their toes by creeping into their shelters at night when they slept, and surrounding them with Anasazi skulls into which he stuck lighted candles. Navajos have an intense distaste for any contact with the dead. Skulls on sticks would not discourage white ex-

Cliff Palace, Mesa Verde National Park, Colorado, may be the best known and most visited of all Anasazi ruins.

plorers, but for years Wetherill managed Mesa Verde and Pueblo Bonito as if they were his private domains, serving as a paid guide to a number of privately financed expeditions.

In 1910, after a quarrel, a Navajo by the name of Chis-Chillings-Begay ambushed Wetherill and shot him through the chest. After Wetherill had fallen from his horse, Begay walked over to his enemy and asked, "What is the matter, Anasazi, are you sick?" He then put the muzzle to Wetherill's temple, shooting him once more through the head. "The skulls have taken their revenge," said the Indians. "You see whose skull is broken now?" "It was not his digging," says a young Navajo, "but his keeping a trading post." Some Indians have a way of dealing with traders who cheat them. A surprising number of traders over the years have died from "lead poisoning" or have had their stores set afire. Even one of the Hubbells, the leading traders, died with a bullet in his body during the 1930s. Today there are some Indian Robin Hoods who will "trash" a trading post, giving some of the loot back to the people, and keeping some for themselves.

Cliff Palace is not the only ruin in Mesa Verde. Crisscrossed by deep canyons, Mesa Verde is an archaeologist's Garden of Eden. Its many ruins show all the different stages of the Anasazis development—from pit houses to cliff dwellings. At first, the people lived on the mesa top, only to withdraw, around 1200, into the forbidding cliffs. "It had taken the Anasazis a millennium," one archaeologist said, "to get out of the caves into the apartment houses, and now, at the height of their achievements, driven by the fear of primitive marauders, the gentle builders found themselves back in the caves."

Some cliff dwellings must have been very difficult to reach, even for the people who made them their home. Nowadays a rope and climbing ability are essential. Studying the handholds and toeholds leading up to a ruin, way above the canyon floor, a Mohawk high-rise construction worker from New York wondered out loud: "Those ancient people, they must have been real mountain goats to get up there. Each one of them would have made a hell of a steelworker." It is indeed hard to imagine women with water jars on their heads climbing these dizzying heights, sometimes by means of a series of ladders that were only treetrunks with notches cut into them.

Ten years ago, when I was skinnier and spryer than I am now, I attempted a similar trail at the back of Acoma Pueblo consisting of a number of very narrow, slanted steps cut into a sheer wall—

Anasazi cliff dwellings were often hard to reach, usually by a series of precarious handholds and toeholds chiseled into the sheer walls. Yet Anasazi women, carrying heavy loads, had no trouble scaling these dizzying trails. Cliff dwellings, obviously, were built for defense.

and promptly froze in my tracks. Yet an old Acoma woman and her grandson ascended the trail as if it were a broad staircase. From their earliest youth the ancient cliff dwellers became accustomed to climbing up and down precarious trails and ladders. For them it was an accepted fact of life. They were as surefooted as squirrels. Examination of their skeletons reveals almost no fractures or other injuries that could have resulted from falls or other climbing accidents.

As Pueblo Bonito and Aztec faded away, Mesa Verde became the center of the slowly shrinking, ingathering Anasazi culture. After the people abandoned the mesa top for the cliffs, every cranny, crevice, cleft, and cave became a refuge. Some cliff dwellings consisted of but one or two rooms, hardly enough to shelter a family.

Others, such as Spruce Tree House, Long House, or Square Tower House, were villages of about a hundred rooms.

To the inhabitants of these little settlements, Cliff Palace was probably looked upon as a kind of capital. Here one could see strangers from far away trading their salt, cotton, turquoise, shells, and obsidian for goods the Mesa Verdans gave them in exchange. Being able to talk to people who had so many tales to tell, so much news to impart, was almost more important than to haggle with them. The cliff dwellers depended to a certain extent on imports. They wove cotton into fabrics, but did not plant it. They seasoned their food with salt brought by outsiders. Dennis Banks, an Indian civil rights leader, once commented on the fact that white people had brought the Indians many things—none of them good. "For twenty-five thousand years," he said, "we Native Americans managed very well without jails, lunatic asylums, police stations, brothels, poorhouses, saloons, or pawnshops."

The whites learned one bad habit from the Indians—cigarette smoking. The Anasazi, as well as the Hohokam and Mogollon before them, smoked cane cigarettes. Among Indians smoking was mainly part of a ritual. In the Southwest today, for instance, members of the Peyote church use corn-husk cigarettes during their ceremonials. Most of the cliff dwellers' tobacco seems to have been imported. The kinnikinick smoked by Indians during their sacred pipe ceremonies, incidentally, is not tobacco, but a healthful red willow bark mixture. Europeans did not learn smoking from the Anasazi, but from Caribbean and South American natives.

Cliff Palace was a town—or a small city-state—of 200 rooms and 23 kivas. It was 3000 feet long, the home for more than 400 Anasazis. The individual rooms were tiny, like monks' cubicles, as one observer put it. The reasons for this smallness were threefold. Space in the cave was limited. Dwelling units had to be kept down in size to make room for everybody; the people were smaller and slimmer

In the case of many Mesa Verde ruins, the plateau with the fields and piñon trees was above the homes of the cliff dwellers, who had to reach them by climbing up handholds and toeholds chipped into the walls.

than they are today. A few inches all around made a big difference in these cramped quarters. A fat person would have been in trouble trying to get through some of the narrow passageways. Finally, the rooms were probably used only for storage and sleeping. The waking hours were spent outdoors—on the little plazas formed by the kiva roofs, in the fields above, on top of the mesa, or below on the canyon floor. Rain or hail was not sufficient to drive the people indoors as the overhanging cave roof covered the settlement.

Fields were owned in common and were alotted to the various families according to need. This had been the custom throughout Anasazi history. It is the custom now. The cliff-dweller period, however, introduced its special novelty: people sought refuge *below* their old homes. They went *up* to tend their fields; they fled *down* in case of danger. Later, the Anasazi would reverse this process. For easier defense, the Acomas and the Hopis built their pueblos at the *top* of inaccessible mesas. They went *down* to plant their corn. If attacked by nomadic enemies, they retreated *upward*.

Contemporary Native Americans talk about "white man's time" and "Indian time." Living on white man's time means being ruled by the clock; fragmentizing the day into hours, minutes, and seconds; being always in a hurry and out of breath.

The Anasazi lived on Indian time—as many Pueblos and other tribes still do—without a clock telling them when to do what. They lived according to nature's natural rhythm, by the setting of the moon, the rising of the sun, the coming of the seasons, the falling of the rains. They needed no alarm clocks. If a man wanted to get up earlier than usual, he drank a little more water before retiring.

Life was regulated by age-old custom; it would continue to be so through coming ages. There were no rulers and no policemen. The wise, old, and holy ones taught the people simply by their example. Through many generations they had learned to get "a feel for the weather." They watched the stars. They told the people when it was time to plant and to harvest. They knew how to forecast the time when a monster would swallow up the sun turning daylight into night, and they knew rituals to bring the sun back from the monster's jaws, making it shed its light and warmth again. Hunting chiefs organized "surround hunts" in which game in great numbers would be driven over a cliff. Corn patches were irrigated and husked corn spread on the roofs to dry.

In the main the cliff dwellers carried on the way of life and customs of the earlier Anasazis. Certain objects found in their ruins establish links to the Pueblos of today. They made *Paho*—prayer sticks—which they placed in the corners of their homes or in sacred places. They used rings of yucca leaves to cushion and hold in place the water jars the women carried on their heads. They painted designs in cornmeal during curing rites, just as Pueblo and Navajo medicine men today use sand paintings in their ceremonies to help the sick. Before eating they put a few morsels of food aside for the spirits of the dead. They used many of the medicinal herbs used by Indians today.

Mesa Verde has its own secrets. What rites, for instance, were performed in the strange structure called the "sun temple"? We do not know who or what was worshiped in it. We do know that it was built by the cliff dwellers, though it rises above ground on the tableland. It was not used as somebody's home. It was in a way a temple devoted to religion, but it is unlike any kiva the Anasazis ever built. D-shaped, double-walled, never roofed-over, perfectly symmetrical, it stands as if erected under the supervision of some priest from a faraway land as a shrine to an alien belief. For all we know—or rather do not know—the sun could have been worshiped in it, or the moon, or the earth. The secret remains.

Like the previous Anasazi sites, the cliff dwellings had been erected in great haste, were lived in, and abandoned within the space of a hundred years. From 1276 to 1299, almost no rain fell. The women had to walk farther and farther in search for water. On the mesa top, the irrigation system collapsed, and the game wandered off. Men still danced and prayed, but the gods had stopped listening and sent no rain. Raiding Navajos and Apaches harried the weakened, despairing Anasazi. And so the people left once more, for a last time, seeking out a great river that would never run dry. Behind them they left their caves and their dwellings with windows like empty eye-sockets, mute witness of their losing battle with the forces of nature. "There may be," says a Hopi elder, "a lesson for all of us here. Man cannot fight nature, he can only adapt himself to her ways, always striving for harmony with the universe. That way there will always be a place for him, a new river to live by. But white men are doing things to the water now, at Black Mesa and elsewhere, which could dry this country up forever, and there won't be anywhere to go then, for Indian or whites."

The cliff dwellers took little with them when they abandoned Mesa Verde except what they carried in their heads and hearts— their skills, their love for the land, and their ancient beliefs. But even as their ancient corn found in a prehistoric jar will sprout again when transplanted to a new field, so the ancient builders would sink new roots in better soil, and with their inborn patience they would build and thrive again.

After the Anasazi abandoned their cliff dwellings and their big apartment house, they went through a stage called Pueblo IV, a time of wandering. Before they finally settled down along the Rio Grande and elsewhere, like the Israelites crossing the wilderness, the Anasazi trekked through the desert, stopping here and there for a spell, and then drifting off again, splitting into a half dozen different language groups, a sure sign of a long dispersion.

Charles Lummis wrote once of "that unique racial chess-playing of the Pueblos, whereof the board was half the size of Europe, and the chessmen were stone cities." The people of Cochiti, for instance, moved their village eight times, "beginning many centuries before history, and ending with the Spanish Reconquest in 1694." This time of wandering is remembered in many legends as a time of purification ordained by the Ones Above.

When the people emerged through the navel of the world, says a Hopi tale, Masauu was there to instruct them that they would have to roam through the land for many lifetimes before they would reach their final destination. To each clan Masauu entrusted a small olla. If they came to a desert they were to put this water jar in the sand and water would spurt from it for as long as they cared to linger. One holy man in each clan was to be in charge of this sacred olla. He would fast and abstain from many things for four days

This early engraving depicts an attack by nomadic raiders upon peaceful Anasazi cliff dwellers.

whenever the people moved to a new place. "Many generations from now," said Masauu, "people will be astonished that you could live for lifetimes here and there in deserts and dry wastelands, because they will not know about this sacred olla which gave you drink during your wanderings." And so the Hopis, step by step, went southward to where they live now.

Farther east, the waters of the Rio Grande acted like a magnet to the many bands displaced by the droughts. But even here the migrations were not made at one jump. On the way to the river the Cochiti people and other Keresan-speaking groups stopped for a few generations in the Rito de los Frijoles—Bean Canyon—in Bandelier National Monument.

As elsewhere, the Indians adapted themselves quickly to their en-

vironment, making it a part of themselves. The cliffs of Frijoles
Canyon, and of the whole national monument, consist of tufa, a
rock so soft that one can dig into it with a spoon. Natural erosion
had eaten many holes and openings into the rock. People simply
widened and connected the many natural openings and passageways
making them into tiny living spaces.

In Frijoles Canyon the Indians built Tiuonyi, a circular pueblo of
four hundred rooms with over a thousand inhabitants; but having
labored on its construction and lived in it for a while, they suddenly
abandoned the place to begin wandering once more.

Lack of water was not the reason for the abandonment of Tiuonyi. Internal dissension might have been the cause. The Anasazi
valued harmony. They arranged their affairs by common consent.
Their was no room for controversy and party strife. Their holy
men were not even allowed to listen to quarrels between clans. If
a disagreement arose during a council meeting, the holy ones would
leave at once. But grave problems arose from time to time, and
these could lead to factions with different ideas about how to deal
with them. If they could not find a compromise solution, one party
had to leave and build a new town elsewhere.

Something like this happened in the early 1900s in the Hopi village of Oraibi. It was split between a "modern" party that wanted
to send their children to a white school, and a "conservative" party
that did not. The only way out of this situation was a "push of
war." A line was drawn through the middle of the village across
which the two factions faced each other. The "moderns" were able
to force their way over the line, pushing the "conservatives" back.
The latter were defeated. They packed up their families and their
belongings, left their village, and built a new town—Hotevila. We
do not know whether something similar happened at Tiuonyi, but
it may have.

The era of migrations, which for some people started in 1300,

After leaving their stone-built cliff cities, the Anasazi settled down in villages along the Rio Grande River, in the process of becoming the modern Pueblos. This is San Felipe in 1899.

and which did not end until 1700, has been called by some archaeologists Regressive Pueblo. "Regressive" meant that the Anasazi culture had declined from the peak attained at Mesa Verde and Chaco Canyon. Some disagree with this word and what it implies. For a few centuries the people were on the move, one clan or band leap-frogging over the other. But the people continued to learn new things, adapting themselves to new conditions and new surroundings. That is why other writers speak of a renaissance, a rebirth, rather than regression, as some early archeologists styled it. The migrations slowed down, the changing of village sites came to a momentary halt. Like pearls on a string, the towns nestled along the life-giving river.

Some towns were laid out according to plan—some rectangular, some in rows and streets, one—Taos—in two building blocks. Some towns shone pink; others were red, brown, white, or honey-colored according to the different shades of stones and clay which varied from site to site. Away from the river, toward the west, stood the fortress rock of Acoma and the Zuñi villages. Still farther west, in the land of the Little Colorado River, huddled the cluster of Hopi hamlets on three arid mesas. There were altogether seventy to eighty villages in the Southwest, each a tiny nation by itself. In the fateful year of 1540 they endured the visit of uninvited guests, strange-looking men mounted on even stranger-looking beasts, men who carried paper, quills, and ink horns with them wherever they went, writing down everything they saw to a faraway ruler, thereby making the Anasazi, by the stroke of a pen, part of modern history.

Suddenly they were no longer Anasazis, but Pueblos; it did not matter to them what historians and archaeologists would call them. Hard-working farmers, the Pueblos went on planting their corn.

# 6 ▪ THE RETURN OF BAHANA

*I came here for gold,*
*not to toil like a peasant.*

HERNANDO CORTEZ

*We came here for the*
*love of god, the glory of*
*the king, and also*
*to get rich.*

One of CORTEZ'S OFFICERS

Those lucky enough to watch a Kachina ceremony—a sacred drama performed by masked dancers—will sometimes see a black monster Kachina with red mouth and red tongue and sharp, white teeth carrying a rattle in one hand and a bow and arrows in the other. It is a mask that scares the children. Of Zuñi origin, this monster Kachina is said to represent "Estevanico, the Moor, the first stranger from across the ocean to come to the land of the Pueblos. The first encounter with men who had sailed to the New World from Europe must have made a lasting impression on the Pueblos; otherwise, there would be no monster to frighten the children more than four houndred years later. Who was Estevanico and how did he come to the ancient Zuñi village of Hawikuh centuries ago?

A Hopi legend tells of Bahana, the lost white brother. Once, mankind had been united. All were of one race, spoke one language. Then Bahana, the white brother, left the people to go east across the Big Water. Before he went, the elders broke a piece off a sacred stone tablet and gave it to him. One day Bahana would come back with many good things and new, useful inventions to help the people. He would bring back with him the missing piece of the sacred tablet, and by this they would know him. And one day Bahana did return, but he was not at all like the people imagined him, and he did not bring back his part of the sacred tablet. He brought new inventions, but also much evil.

Bahana, many Bahanas, had landed in faraway islands in the Caribbean at a time when the Pueblos were still settling along the Rio Grande. But they knew nothing of it. The white newcomers were the Spanish conquistadors, whom many Indians soon called the "bearded mouths." They arrived in ships that looked like huge towers on the water. They came ashore on the mainland, a cross in one hand and a sword in the other. They conquered the Aztec Empire.

*"Oro y plata, oro y plata"*—gold and silver, gold and silver—was all the Spaniards could think about. They dreamed about them in in their sleep. They were looking for worlds to conquer. They conquered Peru and Mexico and were looking for still more lands. Where were these lands to be found?

Estevanico, a Moorish slave, was the first non-Indian, the first stranger from across the ocean whom the Pueblos encountered. He must have made a lasting impression on them. Some say that a certain black kachina represents Estevanico, who so terrified the Zuñis over 400 years ago that they killed him.

In 1536 a gaunt man, skin and bones, with three equally emaciated companions stood in the viceroy's palace. His name was Álvar Núñez Cabeza de Vaca. He had been the treasurer of a large expedition that had been given up for lost since it vanished without a trace eight years before. Cabeza de Vaca was one of several hundred Spaniards who had set out to conquer Florida where they hoped to find both treasure and the Fountain of Youth. He had been shipwrecked, captured by Indians, and had almost starved to death. For years he wandered trying to reach the Spanish outposts in northern Mexico. One of his three companions was Estevanico—Little Stephen—a black slave.

Estevanico has always fired the imagination of historians. He was a colorful, even domineering figure. In the folklore of the Pueblos, he is described as very dark "with lips as red as chile." He picked up languages easily, and had a way with Indian women.

Barefoot and naked, Cabeza de Vaca and his companions struggled through a thousand miles of desolate wasteland "where every plant sticks, stings or stinks." It took them a year to cross Texas. They passed through what is now New Mexico and Arizona, but in the southern part, some two hundred miles south of the Pueblos. They did not see them, but they met many corn-growing Indians who did and who could describe the Pueblos to them with the awe and exaggeration of country yokels talking about a big metropolis. Much of their talk was done in sign language with excited, sweeping gestures which added extra color to their tales. Thus Cabeza de Vaca learned of the Seven Cities of Cibola, big cities with houses three and four stories high, cities larger than the Aztec capital with whole streets full of goldsmith's shops. He saw things that were made in these cities, turquoise necklaces, a cotton shirt. He was given five arrowheads made of emeralds which came from Cibola. Unfortunately, he lost them.

At last came the day when the four men trudging southward into

This picture of the landing of Spanish conquistadors in the New World unwittingly tells the story of early Spanish colonization. The Europeans arrive with the cross in one hand and the sword in the other. They wear armor and carry firearms, while the Indians are naked. Some natives are trying to placate the invaders with gold and silver. Others are running away—probably with good reason.

Mexico found themselves face to face with white men again, and heard again words spoken in Spanish. They had come back to their own people after an incredible journey.

The news of their return spread like wildfire. So did tales about the Seven Cities of Cibola, where the "children played with pearls, diamonds, emeralds and golden toys." It was not Cabeza de Vaca's fault. He was an honest man making an honest report. No, he had not entered Cibola, but he knew that cities were there. He did not know for sure how big and rich they were; but he had seen things that had been manufactured in Cibola which hinted at a high state of civilization. He did not know whether the inhabitants used gold, but he had seen signs that precious metals existed in their country. That was all.

For the Spanish viceroy in Mexico City it was enough to send an expedition there—not a big one, yet. But a scouting expedition was surely warranted. Would Cabeza de Vaca care to lead it? He would not. After his years of hardship Cabeza de Vaca was eager to go home to Spain and to his wife. His two white companions were in no mood for further adventures. That left Estevanico. The black man was once more a slave, a piece of chattel, and the viceroy had obtained title to him. Estevanico became the kingpin of the planned expedition. Who else knew the way? Who else knew the custom and even a few words of the language of those far-off Indians? Estevanico did not object. It was better to be an explorer than a slave.

Of course, it would not do to have a black slave lead an expedition. Luckily, there was a man in town, Fray Marcos de Niza, a French-Italian monk from Nice "versed in cosmography and in the art of navigation, as well as in theology," a bold and enterprising man who had taken part in the conquest of Peru. What better choice to lead the expedition? Fray Marcos was also long on imagination, but that was not yet evident to the viceroy.

And so Fray Marcos, another Spanish monk, Estevanico the Moor, and more than a hundred Indians, among them a number of those who had accompanied Cabeza de Vaca, set out on their journey. It would have the gravest consequences for the Pueblo Indians.

They walked for many weeks, Fray Marcos in his bare feet, according to the custom of his Franciscan order. At Culiacan they left the last outpost of the Spanish Empire behind them.

The black man soon posed a problem to Fray Marcos. He thought himself the better man to lead the expedition—after all, it was *he* who had been Cabeza de Vaca's companion and knew the way. He undermined the monk's authority with the Indian escort. The second friar fell sick and turned back. By himself, Fray Marcos could no longer cope with Estevanico, but he found a way out of his difficulties. He would send the black man ahead as a vanguard, together with some of the Indians. Thus the friar rid himself of the slave who had become a competitor. Before the two commands separated, Fray Marcos instructed Estevanico to send a small cross back—about a hand high—whenever he encountered something interesting. If he came across something really exciting, he was to send back a larger cross—about a foot high. Finally, should Estevanico discover something big and stupendous beyond all expectations—for instance, "a country greater and better than New Spain"— he was to send back a cross as tall as a man. Estevanico was gone four days when a messenger staggered into camp carrying a cross larger than himself. It occurred to Fray Marcos that he had made a mistake. The black slave would be the first to enter Cibola; he would get all the glory. By forced marches the monk tried to catch up, but Estevanico was a hundred miles ahead and moving fast. Fray Marcos had missed out.

From the high rooftop of his house in the pueblo of Hawikuh, a Zuñi chief gazed at a strange procession nearing his village. It was made up of some three hundred Indians of an alien tribe. Had they come to rob and kill? The strangest thing about the band of invaders was the leader, a man unlike any the people of Hawikuh had ever seen. His skin was black. He wore a headdress of deerskin with plumes and horns attached to it. He was wrapped in a many-

In 1536 four gaunt and naked men stumbled into a Spanish outpost in northern Mexico. They were Cabeza de Vaca, two other Spaniards, and a black slave named Estevanico—the only survivors of a large expedition sent out to conquer Florida. They had heard rumors of the fabulous Seven Cities of Cibola—a fancy name for the Pueblo villages.

colored gown which dazzled the eyes. Around his wrists and ankles he wore clusters of small bells which made a tinkling sound whenever he moved. In his hand he carried a feathered medicine rattle. By his side ran two fierce greyhounds. He walked like a man who likes to be obeyed.

The Zuñis were peaceful people, but they would defend themselves when threatened. They did not like to see so many foreigners coming against them with strange weapons. They did not like the black man, obviously a powerful warrior and perhaps an evil spirit, to shake his rattle in their faces demanding—through an Indian interpreter—women, gold, turquoise, and food, and telling them they would be punished if they did not fulfill his wishes. They did not like him threatening them with an army of mighty white men from beyond a great sea who were coming after him. "Tell your chief," said the Zuñi elder to the strange Indians, "that we do not want him here. He must turn back or we will have to kill him."

When he would not listen, they took their bows and shot their arrows at him. Only then did he know that they had meant what they had said, and he ran for his life. But it was too late. So died Estevanico the Moor; and in killing him the people of Hawikuh proved to their satisfaction that he was not a supernatural being from the sky, but just a strange-looking man.

Into Fray Marcos' camp stumbled an Indian messenger, "his face and body covered in sweat." He told the friar that Cibola had been found, but that the Moor was dead. Slowly Estevanico's followers trickled in. The Zuñis had let them go without hindering their flight.

Fray Marcos was stunned. It was the end of his expedition. But he wanted to catch a glimpse of Cibola, even if only from afar. He advanced cautiously until he saw Hawikuh, its red stone and adobe reflecting the rays of the sun. To the monk, the city seemed bathed in gold. He raised a cross and in a loud voice took possession of the land and everything in it in the name of the Spanish king. He then fled, as he himself put it, "with more fear than food," traveling the end stretch at a speed of forty miles a day—in his bare feet.

Back in Mexico City the good monk told the viceroy that the new land in the north was an island, which shows that he was not quite as good a cosmographer and navigator as he thought. He said it was a land in which unicorns lived, which shows him a poor zoologist. He finally said that Cibola, which he had been fortunate enough to see, was the most handsome city in the New World,

Coronado and his expedition first sight Cibola, according to a 19th-century illustration.

fairer and larger than the Aztec capital, that it was a city whose doors were covered with turquoise, where people walked slowly on account of the weight of their heavy, golden jewelry—all of which shows that Fray Marcos also suffered from bad eyesight. The viceroy believed everything Fray Marcos told him, because he wanted to believe.

Gold fever seized the city. It was all true—Cibola existed, richer than Mexico or Peru. The viceroy at once called for another expedition, not a puny affair of a friar and a black slave leading a handful of wretched Indians, but an expedition in the style of Hernando Cortez and Francisco Pizarro. The caballeros flocked to the standard —"many Spaniards poor and greedy, and with a dog's hunger for wealth and slaves."

The conquistadors believed that God was on their side. During a fight they sometimes imagined the Virgin Mary, or Santiago the Moor-killer, their favorite saint, hovering in the clouds over the battlefield, helping them to subdue the pagans. They were convinced that God had created the Indian as a natural slave to serve them. Some believed that Indians had no soul, no brain capable of logic. In their minds, Indians were a commodity with no more rights than a rabbit. It was therefore all right to hunt them down for sport.

Everybody was convinced, from the captain-general down to the lowliest foot soldier, that by a mere waving of the cross and the royal banner, and the mumbling of a few words, one could take possession of the land and all its inhabitants and treasures. Anybody who resisted became a rebel and a traitor who could, and ought to, be killed. In this the Spaniard was not much different in his thinking from other Europeans. But it was the Spanish who had come to this part of the New World and with whom these Indians had to deal.

And so the caballeros assembled to march against the Pueblos. A careful list was made of the men and their equipment. The expedition set out with 230 mounted men, 32 foot soldiers, 4 friars, 1 surgeon, 800 Indians, herds of cattle and pigs, 6 bronze cannons, 27 firearms, and 19 crossbows. Pizarro had conquered the Inca Empire with less.

To lead this expedition the viceroy had chosen Don Francisco Vásquez de Coronado. Not yet thirty, iron-willed and brave, Coronado was a picture-book conquistador. That he was almost broiled alive inside his fine armor in the summer desert was just a little discomfort that a man of his high rank had to bear in patience. Fray Marcos, of course, was his guide.

And so once more the people of Hawikuh saw an army of strangers advancing against them. They looked even more frightening than the black man with the horns on his head. They came riding on large, terrifying beasts. It was hard to tell whether beasts and men were not single creatures, monsters half human and half animal. Their bodies were encased in a shiny, hard material which sparkled

The artist Frederic Remington depicted a typical conquistador—an adventurer on horseback, helmeted, encased in armor, armed with weapons of steel and an arquebus, a primitive firearm that was still effective at short range.

in the sunlight. It did not seem that arrows would be able to penetrate this protective covering. On their heads they wore helmets of the same material topped by bright plumes. They had huge lances, and shields, and strange, clublike sticks. The strangers' skins were white and their faces covered with hair, which was a disturbing thing to see. Their leader, who was more splendidly dressed and equipped than the others, had light hair and eyes as blue as the wondrous metal that protected his body. Could this strange being be human, or was he a god? These white-skinned, half-man and half-beast invaders were accompanied by hundreds of Indians, well-armed and clad in wadded cotton armor. To resist these powerful strangers seemed hopeless.

The old chief drew a line in the sand with a stick. "We do not want war," he said to the strangers, "but if you cross this line we will fight you." The blue-eyed leader understood this gesture. He instantly galloped across the line, and the battle was on.

We must picture the situation in order to grasp the Pueblos' courage.

These were the first horsemen they had ever seen. It was not known whether they were mortal like ordinary men. The huge snorting horses, trampling everything before them, were awe-inspiring. Surely they subsisted on human flesh.

The Spaniards seemed invulnerable. Even some of the horses, driven forward by enormous roweled spurs, wore armor. The strangers' clublike sticks spurted thunder and lightning, which could kill a man at a great distance. Their two-handed swords of steel cut through the Indians' shields of hide and through the arm and bone behind them. The defenders had only stone weapons. The white strangers were horrifying beyond imagination, yet the Zuñis held their ground. They even managed to wound Coronado in the foot with an arrow, so that he lay unconscious while the battle raged. But there could be no doubt about the issue. In a short time Hawikuh fell.

The Spaniards ravaged the village, killing every living thing that got in their way. But they found not the tiniest grain of gold and silver, nor were the doors of the humble adobe dwellings studded with turquoise. "When they saw the first village, which was Cibola, such were the curses that some hurled at Fray Marcos that I pray God may protect him from them. It is a little, crowded village, looking as if it had been crumpled up together."

The starving conquerors swarmed over Hawikuh like locusts: "here we found something we prized more than gold and silver— plentiful corn and beans, turkeys, and salt, better and whiter than I have ever seen." Salt! A poor substitute for pearls and emeralds. But the hope for gold died hard, and the army went on looking for another Mexico or Peru, just beyond the horizon. Nor is that hope dead even now. The Southwest is still a place where prospectors and dreamers keep looking for lost mines and forgotten treasures with as little luck as the unlettered, superstitious conquistadors of old.

Fray Marcos wilted under the scorn of the soldiers. Using sickness as his excuse, he walked back to Mexico, followed by the curses of the army. He lived on in obscurity in some out-of-the-way cloister, the only boon granted him for all his troubles a free ration of wine to soothe his sorrows and his many aches.

Instead of gold and silver, Coronado sent a steady stream of reports back to the viceroy while one of his officers, Pedro de Castaneda, wrote down much of what he saw and heard. On the whole, they were shrewd and alert observations and what they reported shows that the customs and beliefs of the Pueblos of 1540 have not changed much.

About the Zuñis Coronado wrote: "So far as I can find out, these Indians worship water, because they say it makes the corn grow and sustains their life."

He sensed the Pueblos' simple, basic democracy: "As far as I can discover, or observe, none of these towns have a lord, since I have not seen any imposing house by which any superioritty over others could be shown." He recognized another essential Pueblo characteristic: "These Indians love and respect their women more than themselves."

Castaneda also made many valid observations: "The women gather their hair in two lumps above the ears"—in other words, the

In his vain quest for gold, Coronado stormed and burned a number of
Rio Grande pueblos.

famous Hopi "butterfly" hairdo for unmarried maidens was then
widespread. Further: "When a man wishes to marry . . . he has to
spin and weave a blanket and put it before the woman who wraps
herself in it and becomes his wife. The houses belong to the women,
the estufas (kivas) to the men."

Towns there were many, much more than the fabulous seven. In
Coronado's time there were no fewer than seventy Indian pueblos,

and the Spaniards visited most of them. But they did not find them full of gold and silver. Some thought this was due to the native medicine men's sorcery. As one contemporary European author wrote: "The Spaniards have used, and daily use, much diligence in the seeking of treasures, but they cannot find any of them. They say that the witchcraft of the Indians is such, that when they come by these towns they cast a mist upon them so that they cannot see them."

Mist or no mist, Coronado sent parties out in all directions to explore the country. Toward the east went Captain Pedro de Tovar, and Fray Juan de Padilla. They went to the land of Tusayan where they found the cities of the Moquis—the Hopis of today. Tovar had not men enough to try to fight these Indians, but one Spanish patrol went far enough to see and descend into the Great Canyon. The caballeros, however, were not interested in natural wonders.

Coronado also sent captains eastward. It was there, some 150 miles east of Zuñi, that he made his winter quarters in the land of Tiguex, near the modern Bernalillo.

At first the Rio Grande Pueblos welcomed the Spaniards with gifts and the sound of flutes. Said Fray Padilla: "The indians even climbed on the back of each other to reach the arms of our crosses to decorate them with feathers and roses." Maybe they were white men's prayer sticks. The Indians tried to please the Spaniards. The Southwest had a long history of different people sharing a region, even a village, peacefully, but these "bearded mouths" were without pity.

From the Indians' as well as the historians' point of view the Spaniards were raiders and robbers with superior weapons who took from the Pueblos even the humble possessions needed for survival. The people of Alancor were forced to abandon their homes so that white men could live in them. The soldiers seized the Indians' corn which was to feed them during the winter, and as it

Coronado and his soldiers probably were the first white men to encounter buffalo, which they called "Indian cattle." Here is the earliest
European representation of a buffalo.

grew cold they took the cloaks from Indian women's shoulders to
warm their own bodies, driving mothers with babies at their breasts
naked into the snow.

In the village of Arenal a soldier raped a young woman. Arenal
rose against the Spaniards. In a fierce hand-to-hand fight Spanish
cannon fired at short range—forty pieces of stone and jagged iron
with each shot—cutting a wide swath through the ranks of the defenders. After a heroic resistance, the Indians surrendered. They
did not yet know their enemy. The Spaniards planted two hundred
tree trunks in a row, tied their prisoners to them, and burned them
alive. Chiefs from other villages were forced to witness this, to learn
what punishment lay in store for those who resisted.

But the Pueblos found out one more thing. During fights, the

Indians ran off many of the Spaniards' horses, killing them and waving the tails in the Spaniards' faces. The big monsters were not immortal after all!

Sometimes the "bearded mouths" did show pity. On rare occasions when an Indian was to be burned, beheaded, hanged, or shot, the friars would run up to the soldiers with many lamentations, begging that the captive should be released into their care; but "this was not done out of compassion, but to make the Indians believe that the religious were their natural protectors against the men at arms, and to make them trust the priests."

History is written by the victors. The Spaniards wrote much in praise of their knights, but where were the Indians' heroes?

There was a man whose real name or tribe we will never know. The Spaniards called him "the Turk" on account of a turban he wore. This man decided that he would lure the Spaniards away from the ravaged pueblos, even at the sacrifice of his own life. He told Coronado of the kingdom of Quivira whose ruler, Tatarrax, and his nobles ate from golden plates and drank from golden cups in the shade of trees festooned with golden bells. Pack mules, said the Turk, would not be enough to carry all the gold of Quivira away; many big wagons would be needed. So there was a new Peru, a new Mexico beyond the horizon. The Spaniards had just not gone far enough.

Coronado set out to conquer it. The way was long and hard. They marched through parts of what is now Texas and Kansas. They saw many buffalo but little else. After long weeks, they at last reached Quivira—a few grass huts of Wichita Indians around which coyotes lurked. The Indians had no golden plates; they had, as a matter of fact, no plates at all. The Turk had led the conquistadors on an immense wild goose chase in the hope of luring the Spaniards away from the Pueblo villages into the wilderness where, with a little luck, they might perish. "Where is the yellow stone, the gold you have promised us?" asked the soldiers. The Turk laughed in their faces. He was a mighty sorcerer, the Spaniards believed, because one of them had seen him "talking to the Devil hidden in a glass of water." The Turk had fooled them, and Coronado ordered him strangled.

Coronado covered thousands of miles and discovered many towns, but his expedition was a failure. He found no gold. He and his soldiers went home to Mexico.

The "bearded mouths" were gone from the land, and the Pueblos hoped that they had seen the last of them. But this was an idle wish.

# 7 ▪ CONQUEST AND REVOLT

*The Indians fear us so much*
*that on seeing us approach from afar,*
*they flee to the mountains with*
*their women and children, abandoning*
*their homes, and so we take*
*whatever we wish from them.*

LUIS DE VELASCO

For half a century after Coronado, except for a few probing forays, the Spaniards left the Pueblos alone. But they did not forget them. Spain was beginning to run out of conquerors, yet a few glory-hunting men remained eager to astound the world.

One of them was Don Juan de Oñate, described by one writer as "a man of enormous wealth and distinguished lineage with the heart of a beast." Oñate owned silver mines at Zacatecas where hundreds of Indians toiled and died like flies. Their labors made Oñate one of the five richest men in New Spain, but he was also eager for glory. He dreamed of new lands unmeasured, inhabited by unnumbered new subjects to his king. He talked of Holy Church —"to correct the sins and teach these bestial nations." But Oñate was also a practical businessman and iron-handed administrator. He would take all the gold he could find; but, gold or no gold, he would hold the land and settle it.

Oñate was the conqueror come to stay. He was not to be satisfied with bare earth for his bed and a saddle for his pillow. His huge tent housed a campbed, two mattresses, and a prayer stool. In his cape of rose-colored taffeta and his plumed hat, he strutted about as the self-proclaimed future governor of some future province.

Oñate assembled 400 colonists, 100 women and children, 83 lumbering wagons, and over 7000 head of livestock. His wagons were loaded with goods to woo the Indians: combs, tassels for rosaries, glass beads, hawk bells, scissors, toy trumpets, small hats, thimbles and needles. The most cumbersome articles were six large bells for the towers of churches Oñate intended to build, heavy bells that had to be transported over a thousand miles of rough desert country. All this boded ill for the Pueblos.

Oñate was coming by a new route, not by way of the Zuñi villages, but from the south. On April 20, 1598, he reached the Rio Bravo del Norte—better known to us as the Rio Grande. He found a ford, *El Paso del Rio,* and El Paso it has been ever since, the main gateway for all who come up from Mexico.

In solemn ceremony, amid the blare of trumpets, Oñate proclaimed: "On the banks of this Rio del Norte, and in the name of our sovereign lord, King Philip, and of all the saints in heaven, I take possession, once, twice, and thrice, and for all times, and without exception whatsoever, of this kingdom and province of New Mexico, with all its mountains, rivers, houses, gold, silver, copper, mercury, precious stones, together with the native Indians in each and every province, with power over life and death." "And so, with a few mumbled words," say today's Indians, "the white men stole millions of square miles and every living thing moving upon them."

With his caravan of cattle, sheep, pigs, horses, pack mules, settlers, and soldiers, Oñate forded the river. He then faced the forbidding *Jornada del Muerto*—the dead man's journey, a ninety-mile stretch of waterless desert north of the ford. Losing only one man, he reached the land of the Pueblos in an enormous cloud of dust.

Once more, the Pueblos gazed upon a horde of invaders. Oñate summoned the village chiefs and made a long speech ending with these words: "Choose our glorious King Philip for your Lord and salvation, or hellfire everlasting"—fire on earth as well as in eternity, as the Indians had come to know. The Spaniards also fired off their cannon and arquebuses to impress the spectators.

Under conditions such as depicted here, Indians slaved in the mines of Don Juan de Oñate, self-styled conqueror of the Pueblos.

Oñate then parceled out the country to his captains and soldiers, making them gifts of towns, farm and grazing lands, water rights, and native serfs. For himself he took 150,000 acres together with the Pueblos living on them. He had come to civilize the natives. Civilization, the Indians found out, meant taxes. Each Indian household had to furnish one *manta,* about a square yard, of cotton cloth, and one *fanega*—two bushels—of corn each year "wherewith the needy Spaniards could sustain themselves." An example of how these taxes were collected can be shown in 1600, when Captain Zaldivar burned some villages that refused to give him corn, "setting their pueblos

In the early days of Spanish conquest, Indian slavery, while not always legal, was an accepted fact. Indians were hunted with dogs, like animals . . .

. . . branded as a sign of serfdom and formed into slave caravans for the mines and ranches of their Spanish conquerors.

on fire so tactfully and gently that the fire would not cause unnecessary damage beyond what was intended."

While land and tribute went to the soldiers and settlers, the souls were reserved for the friars, each priest being alloted one or another village in which to "harvest his souls." John Upton Terrell has said: "In the unwritten lexicon of the Pueblos, as in the case of every other Indian people discovered by the Spanish, the words *Christianity* and *Christian* were synonyms for *Disaster* and *Death*." This was true at the time of Oñate, even though some friars were gentle, compassionate men who labored faithfully for the welfare of their Indian villagers. Unfortunately, these good friars were in the minority.

Christianization began with the pueblos given patron saints and new names: Santa Clara, Santo Domingo, or San Ildefonso. The villagers went on referring to the towns by their old Indian names, and do so even now. The friars went to work with a will, telling the Pueblos: "We mean to have your souls and we shall get them."

To do the good work there were twenty-six friars for the whole land—"indefatigable in the holy zeal with which they pursued their mission." Within a few years no less than fifty churches had been built; many of them huge buildings laid out in the form of a cross. Some, or at least their ruins, can still be seen. A tremendous amount of Indian labor went into their construction. Pueblo women and children laid the bricks, whitewashed and painted the inside. They built walls four or five feet thick. Men carried the *vigas,* enormous beams to hold the church roofs. The timber sometimes had to be brought on foot from forests thirty miles away. From painted altars new Kachinas looked down on the Indians, images of the white man's saints.

The friars taught the Indians an improved way of building in adobe. They also taught the planting of new crops and the breeding of new animals. They introduced cucumbers, peaches, wine grapes, and brought to the villages strange creatures called sheep, who were

The friars soon built churches everywhere—or rather, they had the
Indians build them.

not only good to eat, but also were covered with thick wool which
could be spun into soft warm garments. The friars' iron tools, everybody agreed, made work easier; "but though the friars did much
that was good, they did more that was evil."

The priests were a law unto themselves. A governor could com-
plain about them, but that was all. Complaints were many: "these
friars use Indian lands for their own private use, make indecent
advances to women, pasture their herds on Indian land, live in the
lap of luxury regarding neither their vows of poverty or chastity,
use the Indians as their slaves and punish them cruelly for slight
faults." Always, whenever a baby was born, or young people mar-

Huge beams for this church at Acoma had to be carried by Pueblo bearers from forests 30 miles distant.

ried, or an old one died, there was the priest, unbidden, sermonizing and sprinkling water; and for this, one had to give something—a haunch of venison, cornmeal, or one's labor.

Worst was the suppression of the Indians' old beliefs and customs which formed such an essential part of the Pueblos' life. The Indians were "forever backsliding into their fiendish practices," as the friars complained. "They dance publicly introducing many superstitious and scandalous acts in these dances, using subterranean places that they call estufas in which they invoke the devil and commit a thousand grievous errors." And so kivas were demolished and sacred masks burned. Men and women were punished for "backsliding,"

The Spaniards believed the Indians to worship many-headed monsters
and live, horned devils. Any means that would make them into good
Christian subjects of the king were deemed justified.

for making a prayer stick, or sprinkling sacred cornmeal, or dancing. For this Indians were whipped "until the bone showed." The
victims could call themselves lucky for not being hanged or burned.

The fifth commandment says: "Thou shalt not kill"; therefore, the
friars shed no blood. A friar could chastise an Indian—as when one
priest beat and burned a Hopi elder with hot turpentine. It was also
all right to work an Indian to the bone and jail him in "a hole not

even suitable for a fair-sized pig." If persuasion and chastising could not make a man forsake his old gods, the friars would simply hand him over to the civil administration for punishment. The Indian would be hanged, or burned at the stake.

As one Spaniard said: "Between the upper grindstone of the caballeros and the lower grindstone of the friars, the Indios were ground down to fine dust." The Indians were forced to lead a double life, a situation which persists to this day. Toward the whites, they behaved like compliant Christians, adopting many of the whites' ways. Inwardly, they remained what they had always been.

The conquest of the Pueblos was not achieved without hard fighting. Colonization bred resistance. The Indians found themselves at a terrible disadvantage. For the Pueblo warrior, a mounted, steel-encased Spaniard represented the same thing a modern tank does to a poorly armed foot soldier. A troop of caballeros were like an armored division, irresistible and invulnerable.

Nor had they, the Pueblos, the advantage of numbers commonly imagined. Their villages were tiny, independent nations, often separated by language as well as miles, and the invaders took them one by one. In the smaller villages there were actually more caballeros than Pueblo warriors. If one adds to this the effect of arquebus and cannon, one wonders that the Indians fought at all. Yet fight they did—and sometimes even won.

An epic battle was fought by the Pueblos of Acoma. The people of the sky city had not sent a cacique to make submission at Oñate's headquarters, but they had sent one spectator who mingled with the crowd keeping his ears and eyes open. His name was Zutacapan. He told his people that the Spaniards were no more than mortal men, that their cannons roared with thunder and belched fire, but that their lightning did not always strike in the intended place. He also told how he saw Indians enslaved by the white strangers. The elders listened. They would not start a fight, but they would not run from one either.

Halfway between the modern cities of Albuquerque and Gallup rises the great rock, the famous Penol of Acoma. Its huge bulk dwarfs the pueblo built on its tabletop, making it look like a toy village. Father Benavides described it as "the Penol of Acoma which has cost so many lives of Spaniards—a chopped-off cliff and inexpugnable because of the valor of its inhabitants." One of Coronado's men had called it "a mesa so high that a shot from an arquebus can hardly attain the top."

The only approach to the summit, four hundred feet above the desert floor, was by way of stairs cut into the rock tapering off into a series of toeholds and fingerholds chipped out of the vertical wall. Oñate himself visited the village on one occasion, scrambling up the dizzying path, escaping death only because, impressed by Acoma's strength, he refrained from any action that could annoy the villagers.

It was different when Oñate's nephew, Captain Juan de Zaldivar, with thirty soldiers appeared at Acoma in December 1598. Don Juan believed "that all the Indios of this country will tremble before ten caballeros in armor." He and his men were hungry and out of food. Their breastplates iced over and their leather jerkins grew stiff with cold. Zaldivar and about half his men inched their way up the steep trail.

Once inside the village, Zaldivar demanded cornmeal and forage for his horses. Some of his soldiers entered houses, pawing the women, grabbing whatever caught their fancies. Infuriated, men and women hurled themselves on the Spaniards, driving them over the edge of the cliff. The whites fought desperately and stoutly, Zalvidar defending himself for a long time with his broadsword. Arrogant and cruel as they were, nobody ever had reason to doubt the Spaniards' bravery.

Five men, rather than face the fury of the villagers, jumped down

Acoma was an ancient city when the Spaniards first saw it. Perched on its 400-foot-high rock, it is possibly the oldest continuously inhabited city in the United States.

from the mesa in an almost hopeless attempt to save themselves. Miraculously, four survived. Stunned by the sudden disaster, the remaining Spaniards spurred on their horses and fled.

Oñate had the news soon enough when one of the survivors gal-

This is what the beginning of the age-old trail to the sky city of Acoma looks like.

loped back to camp. Acoma had handed Oñate his first setback. He could ill afford to lose fifteen men, and even less, to let the dangerous example set by Acoma go unrevenged. He immediately assembled a punitive expedition of some seventy men—all he could spare—giving the command to Vicente de Zaldivar, brother of the slain Juan.

Don Vicente arrived at Acoma in January 1599. His men were

well supplied with powder and lead. Some carried a *pedrero,* a kind of sixteenth-century bazooka fired from the shoulder. They also had two brass culverines, cannon that could be transported on horseback. The Spaniards attended mass and confessed. Then the soldiers advanced, slow-burning matches between their teeth—the glowing ends were put to the touchholes of their arquebuses and pedreros to fire them. The Pueblos, on their part, had gathered great heaps of stones at the edge of the cliffs. These they hurled down on the heads of their attackers, but heavy steel helmets protected the Spaniards. All day the battle raged without either side gaining the upper hand. At nightfall, fighting came to a stop as the men on both sides rested, ate, and slept.

A deep cleft divides the rock of Acoma into two parts. The village is situated on the northern part, the southern part is empty plateau. It was also undefended. A handful of Spaniards discovered a route by which the southern cliffs could be scaled. By the morning of the second day, they had made a lodgement on top, and by means of ropes, hoisted up the culverines.

There remained the cleft. A large tree trunk was found to bridge it, and thirteen soldiers raced across. A small group of surprised Indians tried to stop them. They managed to dislodge the tree trunk so that one end was hanging down into the cleft, and the Spanish vanguard was cut off. At this critical moment, a certain Captain Villagrá took a running jump and vaulted across the chasm. He then managed to work the tree trunk back into place. The Spaniards strengthened their bridgehead and got their cannon across. The Indians had by now been alerted to the danger in their rear. About three hundred of them rushed to the threatened spot, but the culverines were ready for them. Each loaded with pieces of small shot they fired point-blank into the dense mass of warriors, mowing them down in rows. This broke the back of the defense. The Spaniards swarmed into the town, killing all who got in their way—men, women and children. Many Indians committed suicide rather than die by the hands of their enemies, some jumping from the cliffs, others preferring to perish inside their burning homes. At last an old man came to Don Vicente to surrender before all the people in Acoma were dead. So fell the sky city "like valorous Troy of old," as Don Vicente remarked.

The survivors were brought as prisoners to Governor Oñate's headquarters where they were tried for treason. The Indians had many accusers, but not one single defender. Nor could they understand a word of the proceedings. All male prisoners over twenty-five were sentenced to have one foot cut off and to serve the Spaniards for twenty years. All male and female Indians between the ages of twelve and twenty-five were condemned to be distributed among Spanish settlers to labor for them—also for twenty years. Some of the girls were sent to the viceroy in Mexico to be brought up in nunneries. Of course, slavery was forbidden, and the legal-minded governor would never allow it; but punishing rebels and traitors was not slavery by any stretch of the imagination.

This left two men of the Province of Moqui still to be disposed of. These were Hopi visitors who happened to be in Acoma during the siege. The governor, thinking the two had fought alongside the Acoma warriors, said: "I sentence these to have their right hands cut off and to be set free, in order that they may convey to their land the news of this just punishment." In this way the Spaniards were, to use a modern expression, "winning the hearts and minds of the Indians."

The Pueblos saw and listened. They accepted the friars, paid their taxes, and bided their time. The Spaniards "with hearts of triple brass" kept their hands heavy upon the land. As for the Indians, "they must keep crosses over their doors, treat their priests with love and reverence; and, whenever they meet them, kiss the hem of their habit with submission and veneration. None shall dare use horses, or

This early 17th-century engraving shows Spaniards using cannon to subdue Peruvian Indians in battle. Everywhere in the Western Hemisphere, Spanish victories were gained with the help of artillery. This was especially true at Acoma.

the arms of the Spaniards, the which is forbidden by royal ordinances." So read one of the rules of an early Spanish governor.

Oñate eventually went back to Mexico where he was jailed for various misdeeds committed against Spaniards, not Indians.

In 1620 a new governor, Peralta, founded a new capital: Villa Real de la Santa Fe de San Francisco, or Santa Fe for short. It was the only town worthy of the name in the new kingdom, and not much of a town at that. It had a governor's palace, for sure, the Casa Real, now the Presidio, and a large parade ground. But in 1613 it had only 48 white inhabitants, 50 mestizos, and 700 Indian "servants"—15 Indian slaves for every Spanish man, woman, and child.

Between 1600 and 1680 the pueblos were "places where, under the ashes of acquiescence the flame of revolt kept smoldering." The villages lived an uneasy peace punctuated by sudden outbreaks. Though small and local in character, these were straws in the wind—warnings unheeded by the Spaniards. In some cases the Indians practiced nonviolent resistance. In one Hopi town the people resented their forced labor on a huge church which they called a slave temple. One fine day, they packed up to settle elsewhere, leaving their friar an empty village and an unfinished church.

Things went on in the villages of which the Spaniards knew nothing. At night, runners went from pueblo to pueblo whispering and debating, right under the friars' noses. The country, as one Spaniard put it, "was like a great mine beneath the walls of a beleaguered city with a vast train of powder leading to it, wanting only a flame to blow everything asunder."

The Spaniards struck the match. The Indians were now in close daily contact with the white settlers in whose houses and fields they labored, or with the friars who lived in their own midst. Familiarity bred contempt. The whites did not practice what they preached. As one friar said: "The poor, ignorant Indian sees very well what I do and forgets what I say." It was forbidden to give an Indian a horse, or teach him to ride; but it was easier for a Spanish haciendado to send an Indian messenger to a neighbor thirty or forty miles away than to go himself, and faster to put him on horseback. Sometimes horse and rider disappeared. An arquebus was a clumsy and heavy weapon. The forked rest on which to lean and aim the arquebus and the leaden balls were heavy as well. Better let an Indian carry them when one went out hunting deer. Sometimes the Indian ran away, arquebus and all. But one did not talk about such things to one's neighbor.

The Spanish rule had meant genocide for the Indians. By 1680 their numbers had sunk to half of what they were when the white men first arrived. Some villages, such as Pecos and Acoma, had been decimated by war. Others were ravaged by the white man's diseases against which the Pueblos had no inbred immunity. Some villages starved in times of scarcity when the soldiers took their corn to feed themselves. Many villages ceased to exist altogether, having been abandoned by the despairing inhabitants. The Spaniards had so churned up the land, driving the people from one village to take refuge with their neighbors, that they themselves had broken down the isolation in which the tribes had lived up to then.

From 1668 on, droughts and famine repeatedly hit the province. It would not be the Spaniards who were hit hardest. In one pueblo, five hundred died of hunger. The roads were littered with corpses. The Pueblos began to think it was better to die as a rebel than to die as a slave. The Indians also thought that they had fared better under their old gods than under the new god of the Christians. Men again openly made prayer sticks, while women sprinkled sacred cornmeal. The holy water of baptism was washed away with yucca suds. From the kivas, once more rose the sound of voices singing and the beat of pulsating drums.

In 1675, therefore, the governor ordered "all superstitious practices" to be rooted out. Denounced by the friars, forty-seven medicine men and Indian religious leaders were arrested as witches and tried for sorcery. Three were hanged, the rest flogged until their flesh came away in shreds, then jailed. Among these was a medicine man named Popé from the Pueblo of San Juan, a "man of the sort best treated fairly or killed." He was neither. After the medicine men had languished in their prison for some time, a delegation of seventy Pueblo leaders appeared before the governor at Santa Fe demanding the release of the prisoners—and not humbly either. They threatened that their people would leave their villages and join up with the wild Apaches unless the men were freed.

At this time there were 2500 Spaniards in all of New Mexico, and 30,000 Pueblos. Of fighting men, the governor had only 150 at hand, among whom were 46 convicts who were sentenced to settle in Santa Fe instead of being jailed. The province was described as a "barbarous, miserable kingdom where caballeros do not live much better than the ragged Indios, where the religious and the officers never cease to dispute with each other, where in the whole ill-defended town, there is not one place where a person can decently relieve himself." The governor was not in a position to argue. He released the prisoners. Popé did not go back to San Juan but fled to Taos, the northernmost pueblo. He was welcomed by the village elders, then settled down in a kiva like a mountain lion licking his wounds.

Popé was a remarkable man, charismatic leader, a good planner, and an organizer. He was a gifted statesman and clever politician. He had what the Indians call "medicine power." He was the right man at the right time to lead the Pueblos against the Spaniards, yet he was not a fighting chief, a Geronimo or a Crazy Horse. He was instead another Sitting Bull, a holy man and prophet who used his spiritual power, rather than a war club as his weapon.

The little we know of him comes to us from the Spaniards, in whose eyes he was not merely an enemy, but an archfiend and sorcerer helped by devils and demons. Popé lived in a different world from theirs; he did not fit into their conventional image of a conventional enemy. They did not know how to deal with him. It was less wounding to the Spaniard's pride to paint him as a savage witch doctor who defeated them with the help of black magic than to admit that he outthought and outgeneraled them.

We can know more of Popé by looking at his deeds than by looking into Spanish history books, and his deeds speak for themselves. He was the first Indian in North America to unite many tribes in a successful war of resistance against white invaders, to win a victory, to die free and undefeated. He was not soft or meek or humble. He was a good hater. He wore the scars of Spanish whips on his back to remind him of his hate. His message to the Pueblos was unity, steadfastness in their age-old religion, and resistance. His was a simple message and it spread like wildfire. The width and breadth of the land—from Taos to the Hopi villages—heard that message.

The great Pueblo revolt of 1680 has been called "New Mexico's best kept secret until the atomic bomb." It must have been planned for a long time. It was prepared and organized by men who had to communicate with each other on foot over distances of hundreds of miles, between pueblos speaking different languages, right under the noses of the friars residing in almost every village. The secret must have been known to every Indian in the land, yet the Spaniards were kept in the dark until the last moment. They did feel a certain tension in the air. Even the thick-skinned caballeros sensed that they were living surrounded by a sea of Indian hostility. The governor, Antonio de Otermin, reported to the viceroy in Mexico that he thought the Indians were up to no good. He also asked for reinforcements, new soldiers, new settlers, arms and money. But he did not get them.

Meantime, Popé had finished his preparations. He had a vision that it was time to strike. From Taos—"the womb of rebellion"—he sent to all pueblos messengers carrying knotted cords. Every day one knot was to be untied. As soon as the last one was loosened the people were to attack the Spaniards. Thus, the day of liberation was fixed. It was, according to the white man's calendar, August 11, 1680.

On August 9, two Christian converts from the pueblo of Tesuque appeared before Governor Otermin saying that they had heard about an uprising to take place soon. They were not in the plot and were not aware of its extent, but they knew about the cords. There were

In 1680 all the villages rose in the great Pueblo revolt, driving the Spaniards from their country.

only two knots left untied. It never occurred to Otermin that he was facing a whole country united in a common cause. He could not credit the Indians with the organizational skill that would induce all the villages to bury their differences and act on a common plan. He probably expected some trouble from one or two villages. But he alerted the capital, strengthened its defenses, and sent warnings to haciendas and settlements he thought might be threatened.

News of these measures swiftly reached Taos, and Popé knew that the revolt had been betrayed. Not wanting to give the Spaniards any more time to get ready he reacted boldly, ordering the uprising to begin the next day. We do not know by what superhuman efforts he managed to advance the attack. He had only runners to communicate his orders. We can only imagine that the swiftest young men of Taos ran throughout the night until their lungs and hearts were ready to give out—stumbling into villages by some back road, unseen by priests or Spanish patrols—and panted out their message so that other young men could carry it a village farther.

On August 10, the Pueblos rose as one, killing all the Spaniards they could lay hands on. In Taos, Picuris, Nambé, Santo Domingo, Pecos, Sandia, Galisteo, Jemez, Acoma, San Ildefonso, and elsewhere, the war chiefs assembled their fighting men with their lances, clubs, and shields of leather, their quivers full of new arrows. Priests were slain before the altars of their churches, haciendas were wiped out. Here and there one could see a Pueblo warrior wearing a breastplate or helmet conquered in hand-to-hand combat, waving a caballero's sword, riding a Spaniard's horse. One out of every five Spaniards in the country died on that day. For many years the Spaniards had sown the wind; now, at last, they were reaping the whirlwind.

Over a thousand refugees straggled into Santa Fe. As the bad news continued trickling in, Otermin had to face the fact that the whole country had risen against the Spaniards. He was now in frantic haste to prepare the city against the storm he knew would come at any moment. Women helped to dig ditches and put up earthworks. Friars molded lead bullets. Men knelt before priests confessing their sins, which were many. Cannon stood ready, loaded to the muzzle. The soldiers stood by to apply their lighted matches to the touchholes. Otermin did not have long to wait. On August 14 a force of about five hundred Pueblo warriors approached the city. They were led by such men as Luis Tupatu, from Picuris, not by Popé, who was not a man of war but a prophet. Among the Indians was a giant black slave who had run away from his master to hide among the people of Taos—a man about whom the history books have nothing to say.

Otermin was dismayed to see that a few Indians carried arquebuses captured from the Spaniards. He also recognized among the besiegers a leader whom he knew—Juan of Galisteo. From the roof of the palace, the governor shouted to Juan to come and negotiate, offering him safe conduct. Juan came willingly because he wanted to speak to the governor. When they met, Otermin reproached the Indian with bitter words. "Juan," he said, "how could you, a Christian and one who speaks our language, do this thing, rebelling against Holy Church and your rightful king?"

Juan listened politely. He had not come to argue. "My people have chosen me for their captain," he said simply. "There is no need for us to kill each other. All we want is for you to go away. Here, I have brought two crosses, a white one and a red one. Choose the white one as a sign of peace, hold it while you march out with your people and wagons. We will not harm you or stop you. Or choose the red one which means war."

"It is not too late for a full pardon," said the governor. "Return to obedience now, and each and every one of you will be forgiven."

Juan answered that the Spaniards were very good at making promises but very bad at keeping them. When the governor asked how the Indians would get along without their priests, Juan answered "You must choose now." Otermin would not take the white cross, so Juan put the red one on a table before the governor, went out of the palace, mounted his horse, and rode away "holding his seat as well as any Spaniard."

On the next day the Indians set up a great shout of war, rang the bell of the church of San Miguel, and set fire to it. They then met the Spaniards in battle. The fight raged all day in various places in and out of the city. The Spaniards realized they could not hold the city. They decided to make their stand in and around the Casa Real, the palace, which at that time had two towers. On one of them, Otermin planted his large royal banner of yellow silk. The Indians then swarmed into Santa Fe setting fire to the houses, probably thinking of the many Indian villages the Spaniards had burned. "On that day the whole city became a flaming torch."

By August 16, the Indians had been reinforced by men from Taos, Tesuque and Picuris, swelling their numbers to over two thousand. We do not know whether Popé or the war chiefs made the wise decision not to storm the castle by force, but to defeat the Spaniards by cutting off their sole water supply, an irrigation ditch leading from the Santa Fe River to the palace. Fighting went on most of the day, the Indians repulsed at the palace, the Spaniards at the ditch. The battle continued the next day when Otermin was wounded in the chest and saw five of his soldiers killed. Otermin had had enough. His men and animals half crazed with thirst, he took his silken banner down from the wall and marched out of the city in as good an order as was possible. He did not even have enough horses for his sick and wounded. The beaten conquerors drove their whole living food supply along the road before them—a few miserable goats and sheep. This happened on Sunday, August 20, 1680. Stoically the Indians watched in silence from the rooftops of the few undestroyed houses. They did not try to interfere with the retreat. The long battle of Santa Fe was over. That night the Kachinas danced in the plaza of Santa Fe. "The white man's god is dead," said Popé. "He was only a piece of wood."

Otermin's disheartened column limped south toward safety, marching through the silently hostile land "as between the walls of enemy cities." In one pueblo they found the bodies of eight Spaniards, but the church undisturbed, the altar with its chalices and candle-

In the course of the great revolt, almost all Spanish churches were destroyed.

sticks untouched. On his march, suddenly and very much too late, it occurred to the governor to stop single Indians along the road to ask them: "*Why?* Why did you rise against us?"

One old man said: "We were worked like animals by the padres, driven by the whip, so that we had no time to plant for ourselves." Another Indian said his people had become tired of the endless slave-work they had to do for the settlers as well as the friars, "and seeing no other way out of their troubles, they rebelled." Asked the same question another old villager answered simply: "Because you would not let us live in the way of our ancestors."

The various groups of Spanish survivors joined up with a few hundred "loyal" Indians, mostly from Isleta. They lost no time in putting the desert between themselves and the Indians. They did not stop until they had crossed the Rio Grande, coming to a final halt at El Paso—the modern Juarez—and "this town and settlement was all that was left to us of the kingdom and province of New Mexico." For ten years no living Spaniard remained in the land of the Pueblos.

After their great victory Popé and the other chiefs ordered the people to bathe in the river to wash away baptism and Christian ways with yucca suds. Everywhere kivas, destroyed by the Spaniards, were rebuilt, churches demolished, the images of saints burned. Popé decreed that nothing of Spanish origin remain. Peach trees were felled, wheat fields uprooted. Pigs were slaughtered and horses released into the wilderness. Maybe this was the birth of the great herds of wild mustangs which quickly spread north, changing forever the lives of the Plains Indians.

Popé now ruled a country of united pueblos from the Casa Real, the palace in Santa Fe, to Taos in the north. It was the first attempt to form an all-Indian intertribal government. He ruled the country not like a king but like a priest. He was not a remote figure but was constantly visiting villages on his black mule wearing a headdress adorned with a huge buffalo horn, which seemed to come out of his forehead.

The Spaniards describe Popé as having waxed arrogant and haughty, saying that "the Indians thought that his rule was worse than a Spaniard's." But no white man could know this, because none were left in the country. What they wrote down, long after Popé was dead, they heard from Indians who had learned to tell the whites what they liked to hear. Certain only is that Popé died in 1688. His unique personality had held the federation together. With his death it fell apart. A strong government with one ruler, even a holy man and prophet, was, after all, not the way of the Pueblos, the world's natural democrats. And so the Pueblos lived as they had always lived, in the words of Governor Otermin, "very happy without priests or Spaniards."

The Spaniards, naturally, did not like to lose their province. Successful rebels could set a bad example. The Spaniards therefore decided to reconquer New Mexico. The man chosen for this task was Don Diego de Vargas, then forty years old, indefatigable and of spare frame, a man described as "proud, haughty, confident." In August 1692 the noble governor—El Reconquistador—set out on his mission with the usual lengthy ceremonies.

After almost 150 years of battling Spaniards, the Pueblos were weakened and weary of war. If Don Diego would be satisfied with token submissions, they were ready to humor him. They also used a sort of scorched-earth policy against the Spaniards. As the caballeros approached, the Indians simply took to the bush together with their food supply, leaving only empty villages in the path of the invaders.

But the Indians in Santa Fe neither fled, nor opened the gates of the city to Don Diego. The governor rode up to the adobe walls shouting up to the Indians looking down at him from the flat roofs, "speaking sweetly of peace and pardons," telling the Indians that "the old, bad governors are dead and gone." "Yes, but will the new ones be any better?" asked the men on the rooftops, letting Don Diego cool his heels before the city. He then did what the Indians had done to the Spaniards: he cut off the town's water supply. Nobody wanted a fight, especially Don Diego, who had slender forces to back him up. He and Tupato of Picuris, the Indians' chief, came to terms over a cup of chocolate. The defenders would let the Spaniards in and would acknowledge themselves good Christian subjects to the king. The governor would not press matters further but go on to gather other subjects elsewhere. This was done with much trumpeting and waving of flags.

Don Diego marched on, his friars persuading, baptizing, and sanctifying marriages. At Acoma, the people would not let him up, neither would they come down. They shouted their submission from the mesa top and that had to suffice. At Zuñi, the governor found the only traces of the Christian faith, a few tattered vestments and a cross left over from before the revolt. At the great white rock called "El Morro," that "giant autograph album made of stone," the governor carved his own message into the cliff: "Here was General Don Diego de Vargas who conquered for our Holy Faith and the Royal Crown all New Mexico at his own expense in the year 1692." His inscription is still there for all to see, and so is an older one by Oñate. But had Don Diego really conquered? Not yet. He went to the farthest limits of the province, to the Hopi villages, and then marched back across the Rio Grande, happy to have baptized two thousand Pueblo children.

In the fall of 1693 Don Diego de Vargas was back before Santa Fe; but he was no longer the soft-spoken, all-forgiving man of the year before. Now he had come with 100 soldiers and 800 armed settlers. They had new weapons, too—newfangled flintlocks and muskets which could shoot faster and farther than the old arquebuses. He also had three large fieldpieces that could do the talking now.

When the Indians refused to give up their homes to the settlers, Vargas stormed the town. The Pueblo chief committed suicide. The Indians who surrendered soon found out that they had made a mistake. Seventy were hanged; 400 others, among them many women and children, were given to the Spaniards as "servants." Vargas proceeded to reduce the pueblos one by one with fire and sword. A glimpse of the governor's character could be had when he forcibly baptized an Apache only to have him immediately hanged "as a good Christian horsethief, giving him a gentle death." And so, in his own way, Don Diego brought "civilized ways" back to the Pueblos.

In 1694, shouting "Santiago, Santiago, death to the rebels!" the army stormed Jemez, killing 84 Indians and putting 300 women and children into servitude. The village food and cattle were given to the padres to found a new mission. The Spaniards also took the women and children of San Idlefonso prisoner, telling the men that they would have to help the soldiers subdue the other villages if they wanted their loved ones back. Many Indians took refuge on top of the Black Mesa of San Idlefonso where they held out for nine long months.

The Pueblos fought back desperately for almost four years, but they could not resist forever the power of the mighty Spanish Empire. The soldiers and settlers were steadily reinforced from Mexico to make good their losses. Whole villages disappeared from the map. The inhabitants of one fled all the way to Tusayan where they built a new pueblo, called Hano among the Hopis.

In 1696 occurred one of the last revolts, in which twenty-one Spaniards and five padres were slain. Law and order, Spanish style, returned to the land as the Pueblos finally gave up the fight. Shooting, cutting, and hacking were never their way anyhow. War was the Spaniards' way. The Pueblos would find another way to survive.

The new, reestablished Spanish order did not extend as far as it had before. The Spanish settlers restricted themselves wisely to the Rio Grande valley south of Taos. When this part of the country was pacified and Don Diego had successfully done his butcher's job, a new governor came out and promptly relieved him. The age of revolts and conquistadors was over.

There was one great difference between the Southwest before and after the great revolt. The Spaniards, as well as the Indians, saw that a way must be found for kiva and church, kachina and saint, to coexist. Otherwise, the cycle of revolt and repression would go on

The palace of the governors, once besieged and taken by Indians during the great Pueblo revolt, now a place where Indian arts and crafts are sold.

endlessly. The church lost much of its rigidity. Kivas were no longer burned, or medicine men whipped and hanged. A live-and-let-live spirit developed. Among modern activist Native Americans, a sellout, a yes man, an "uncle tomahawk," is often called an "apple": red outside, white inside. The Pueblos learned to be the opposite—white and Christian outside, Indian inside. To the uninitiated outsider, the two religions seemed to blend. Scratch Pueblo Christianity a little bit, and the old faith of the Anasazi began to show. And so it remains today.

In 1894 an observer of the southwestern scene, Matilda Stevenson, summed it up:

The Pueblos are in fact as non-Catholic as before the Spanish conquest, holding their ceremonies in secret, practicing their occult powers to the present time, under the very eye of the Church. The Catholic priest marries the betrothed, but they have been previously united according to their ancestral rites. The Romish priests hold Mass that the dead may enter heaven, but prayers have already been offered that the soul may be received by Sus-sis-tin-na-ko, their creator, into the lower world. Though professedly Catholic, they await only the departure of the priest to return to their ancient ceremonials.

After 1700 the Spanish Empire went into decline. For years it had sent forth its sons, until Spain itself was underpopulated, and still it had not been able to fill its vast overseas possessions with settlers. Spain became a second-rate power in Europe's back yard. New Mexico, became known as the sick province of a sick empire. Many Spanish colonies declared themselves independent. Mexico became an empire, then a republic. The Pueblos became part of Mexico. To the Indians it made no difference. Mexico was even less able to settle and develop the country. Already in the north loomed a new, young, lusty, greedy, land-hungry giant, an altogether different kind of white man, willing to fill the void which Spain had left.

In 1811 a Spanish traveler lamented: "Oh Indians of old, now you belong to history alone and your remains are sure to perish soon." It did not occur to him that it was his own empire which was about to perish.

D. H. Lawrence was wiser when he wrote about the Pueblo villages: "That they don't crumble is a mystery. That these little squarish mud heaps endure for centuries after centuries, while Greek marble tumbles asunder, and cathedrals totter, is a wonder. But then, the naked human hand with a bit of new, soft mud is quicker than time, and defies the centuries."

# 8 ▪ A DIFFERENT KIND OF WHITE MAN

*Our rapid multiplication will expand and*
*cover the whole continent with a*
*people speaking the same language,*
*governed in similar forms and*
*by similar laws.*

THOMAS JEFFERSON

One day, around 1810, a strange, wild figure of a man rode his horse into the village of Taos. He was gaunt, hawk-eyed, and hawk-nosed. His long hair and beard were matted, and the fringed and beaded buckskin hanging loosely about his spare frame had soured on him. On his head he wore a low-crowned, wide-brimmed hat. Across his saddle he carried the most important piece of his equipment—a heavy, muzzle-loading Hawken rifle which could bring down a buffalo at a range of 150 yards. Stuck in his belt was a pistol and a skinning knife with a fourteen-inch blade. Among his other possessions were half a dozen beaver traps.

This fierce apparition was the forerunner of a new breed of men—the white English-speaking invaders of the north, the mountain men and free trappers who went west in search of beaver pelts. They were the first *gringos,* or Anglos, to come to the land of the Pueblos. They were an ornery, solitary lot, as hard as the steel of their traps, men who needed a whole continent for elbow room. They were a law unto themselves, all of them the epitome of the white American West's free frontier spirit.

They were not fastidious. They ate anything that came their way. The raw liver or the intestines of a buffalo were delicacies to them. It is strange that these fierce, incredibly hardy Kentuckians, Virginians, Yankees, Scotch-Irish, and French Canadians came to

The first white North Americans, or so-called Anglos, the Pueblos
encountered were a strange breed. They were the mountain men,
trappers and trail-blazers, fantastically garbed, untamable, and highly
individualistic.

the land of the Pueblos at the whim of effeminate dandies in faraway London who had created a new fashion in men's wear—the
celebrated beaver hat.

The American West was the only place where beaver could still
be found in great numbers, and so the shiftless, the wild ones, men
who boasted that they were half timber wolf and half alligator, went
West, walking every trail, trapping every stream, traveling incredible distances. They ranged from the Canadian to the Mexican
borders, and from the Missouri to the Pacific. They drifted into

the Southwest trapping the side streams of the Rio Grande, the Gila River, and the Colorado River. They came into Mexican territory like a plague.

By this time the conquering days of the Spaniards had been long gone. Once mighty Spain had become a poor, underpopulated country in the backwaters of Europe, Mexico proclaimed its independence. But neither Spain nor Mexico had the strength or people left really to settle the country. This was dangerous, because beyond this wilderness loomed the United States, its people bursting with a furious, restless energy to fill the continent from sea to sea.

Of course, even a weak government will try to protect its borders and insist that they be respected. The Spanish government did insist, and the Mexicans later on. But most of the time, the Santa Fe authorities were powerless to stem the tide, and behind the mountain men was the great mass of land-hungry, silver-hungry, grasping, industrial *Norte Americanos*. They were like rambunctious children forever outgrowing their clothes, always on the march, a new empire pushing aside an old one.

Taos fell more and more under the influence of the mountain men—white Taos that is. There were now two villages of that name: the Spanish outpost, San Fernando de Taos, a few stores and cantinas, a handful of officials and soldiers; and the Indian pueblo two miles away. Both villages were affected by the coming and going of the trappers.

Taos was situated in  good beaver country. It was not much to look at, a tiny plaza and a few crumbling adobe structures. But to the mountain men, it was a great metropolis. Behind them stretched a million square miles of wilderness. Taos was the only place where a man could buy or trade for some coffee, sugar, and flour; where he could obtain powder and lead, ribbons, beads, and other "foofaraw" for his "squaws"; where he could bathe in a barrel of hot water, get a meal of chili, and plenty of raw whiskey—the infamous

Taos was a town where the white man could buy tobacco and whiskey.
Here he could gamble, dance the fandango, and find women.

"Taos Lightning which struck a man on the spot." It was a place
where one could hear the sound of fiddles and guitars, and where
the lone trapper, after a long season in the wilderness, could find a
willing mestizo woman to dance the fandango with.

Under the impetus of the fur trade, Taos became a meeting place
where Mexicans and Anglos, plains Indians and Pueblos, came to
barter. As a result of this commingling, the Taos pueblos received
many articles of North American manufacture and adopted some
of the ways of the Plains tribes. Unlike the men from other pueblos
they braided their hair and walked around wrapped in blankets.
Their songs and dances were influenced by the Plains culture, and
they became as skillful in riding and hunting as their northern
cousins.

The mountain men loom large in the history of the West, twice
as large as life, but their time was short. They flourished for a mere

Early days in Santa Fe—after New Mexico became a part of the United States.

generation—until about 1840 when the beaver was largely trapped out and a man in England invented a process for making hats out of felt.

After the trappers came the traders. They came down the famous Santa Fe Trail from Independence, Missouri, and Fort Leavenworth, Kansas, a long, hard, rutted road of eight hundred miles for the Yankee and Saint Louis merchants to travel to make a dollar. The gringos carried no cross; they did not claim to come in the name of God or a king. They just wanted to make a profit. Most of the goods sold at Santa Fe had until then first come from Spain to Vera Cruz, and from there overland to New Mexico. Yankee goods traveled a shorter route with less red tape. They were not only cheaper, but also better and more varied.

With the traders came the first tourists, pale men suffering from lung disease and other troubles who undertook the journey in the pure, dry air of the high prairie "for its sanative effect," hoping it would cure them. In some cases it did. They all found Santa Fe slumbering in "incredible remoteness," and the town was still much as it had been in the days of Diego de Vargas.

In this city of three thousand lived many Indians from different pueblos. They now had a chance for their first good look at these pale strangers who did not worship the images of saints, who spoke a different language and wore different clothes than the Mexicans.

The traders were no lovers of the Indians. In the words of Josiah Gregg, himself one of them: "Many seemed to forget the wholesome precept that they should not be savages themselves because they dealt with savages." Instead of cultivating friendly feelings Gregg said, there were occasional traders always disposed to kill, even in cold blood, every Indian that fell into their power. The strangers' attitude boded no good.

It was not long before the enterprising newcomers dominated the economy. Their goods soon became indispensable to Mexicans and Indians alike. At the same time more than twenty thousand Americans had settled in Texas, becoming a sizable part of the population. The Anglos became a dominant influence in parts of the Southwest—economically, militarily, and numerically. In 1845 the United States admitted Texas to the Union, thereby provoking Mexico to declare war and to send a force across the Rio Grande. It was repulsed. In 1846 Congress, in its turn, declared war on Mexico.

An American army under Brigadier General Stephen Kearny marched from Fort Leavenworth to Santa Fe. The Mexican governor, Armijo, known as "His Obesity," gathered about four thousand men, more than twice as many as Kearny had, but all untrained and badly armed. Many were Pueblos who showed little enthusiasm helping one army of whites against another. Armijo was persuaded to withdraw without risking a battle. On August 19, 1846, the Stars and Stripes waved over the old governor's palace. As a result of the

The Spaniards and Mexicans had come in a trickle, the Anglos settled in swarms. They first came by oxcart . . .

. . . or by horse and buggy.

war, Mexico ceded to the United States half its territory, one million square miles, all of New Mexico, Arizona, Nevada and California, as well as parts of Colorado and Wyoming. The land of the Pueblos had a new master.

The Pueblos would have liked to ignore them, but this was not easy. The Anglos were very different from the Mexicans. They were forever busy and at work changing the land. In the wake of their soldiers came a stream of immigrants, officials, administrators, businessmen, surveyors, lawyers, judges, cattlemen, miners, farmers. The western pioneer has always been treated as a folk hero, a bringer of civilization. The Indian, and some white men, saw him in a different light. The famous western painter, Charles M. Russel, said he was a sonofabitch who hunted out the land, trapped out the valleys, fished out the streams, cut down the trees, fenced in and dug up and plowed under the earth, robbing it of its treasures. There could have been no greater difference than that between the life styles of the Pueblos and these Anglos.

On August 30, 1846, chiefs of many pueblos came to Santa Fe to pledge allegiance to their new overlords. They were described as "a fine, hardy, robust-looking set, with bows and arrows and Indian dress." The American commandant reported that "300 years of oppression had failed to extinguish in this race the recollection that they were once the peacable and inoffensive masters of the country." Another American said of the Pueblos: "A more upright and useful people are nowhere to be found." There were many fair words and promises exchanged, but it was action that counted.

Americans, coming armed into a new country, always see themselves as liberators, as the bringers of democracy and of Yankee know-how. They expect to be liked and appreciated, and take it amiss if they are not. The fact was that the Pueblos did not like these new, brash Anglos, and there was no reason why they should.

They had not liked the Spaniards or Mexicans either; but at least they had come to know and get used to them. There is an old saying that the government is best which governs least. The Mexicans had done very little governing. Most of the Hopis never saw a Mexican official. The padres had long ago learned to close their eyes to the practice of the old Indian religion and its rituals, the church being quite content with a little outward show of Christianity.

The Anglos meant to govern. They wanted things done their way. The northern pueblos, especially the Taos people, were afraid of them. They had seen the mountain men get drunk and fight with each other with knives and guns over a woman or a beaver pelt. They had seen Indian scalps hanging from their belts. They had learned to despise the Anglo traders who so often cheated them. The Mexicans, who tried to stir up the population against the new rulers, frightened the Pueblos further by telling them that the *Diablos Americanos*—the American devils—would take their land and their faith away.

When two cultures and two races encounter each other for the first time the resulting clash often ends in disaster. At Taos, this proved true. An Indian was arrested on a charge of treason. It is hard to see how an Indian could commit treason against a government that did not recognize him as a citizen and that he in turn did not recognize. The Taos people asked for the man's release. Their demand was refused. The Pueblo rose in revolt.

On August 19, 1847, Taos men broke into a house in which the newly appointed governor of New Mexico, Charles Bent, was staying. They shot him with bows and arrows. They killed another dozen Americans but did not touch the white women and children, though these would later testify against them.

The Americans gathered a force of 350 men under Colonel Sterling Price, for what was called a punitive expedition. On a bitterly cold

Tragedy struck at Taos when its inhabitants rose against American rule. In this Taos church the Indian defenders took their last stand. It was bombarded with howitzers and stormed by bayonet-wielding soldiers. Fighting bravely, 150 Indians died inside.

winter day, under a pale sun, they entered the pueblo. Not a soul was to be seen. Many of the people had taken sanctuary inside their thick-walled adobe church. Colonel Price gave them a foretaste of modern war. Four howitzers bombarded the church. The defenders fought with the courage of desperation, but at last a breach was made in the wall wide enough for five or six men abreast to enter. Then the Indians experienced a new kind of horror—hand grenades.

The dragoons were holding the bombs in their hands until the fuses were nearly burned and then tossing them inside to do their work of devastation.

One hundred and fifty Taos people were slain, and twice as many wounded at the cost of ten fallen soldiers. An eyewitness, Lewis Garrard, describes the scene after the massacre:

We entered the church at the breach through which the missiles of death were hurled. We silently paused in the center of the house of Pueblo worship. On either side the lofty walls were perforated by cannon balls, strewed and piled about the floor. Climbing and jumping over them, we made our way to the altar, now a broken platform, with scarcely a sign or vestige of its former use; and in the room behind it we saw where the defenders, after a determined struggle, bravely met their certain fate.

About the fate of the Taos people, the same writer reported sadly:

A few half-scared Pueblos walked listlessly about, vacantly staring in a state of dejected, gloomy abstraction, and they might well be so. Their alcalde dead, their grain and cattle gone, their church in ruins, the flower of the nation slain or under sentence of death, and the rest—refugees starving in the mountains.

Colonel Price had promised to spare the lives of the survivors if the "ringleaders" would surrender. They did. One of them was hanged outright after a drumhead court-martial. The others were tried for murder or treason. "Treason indeed!" wrote the same witness. "What did the poor fellow know about his new allegiance? I left the room sick at heart."

First six, and then nine prisoners were hanged. They drew their blankets around themselves and marched to their deaths with dignity. It was Good Friday, the day of crucifixion. And so Taos had become a part of the United States.

Fortunately Taos was the only battle the Pueblos had with the Americans, who from then on did their fighting against the nomadic Plains tribes, the Navajos and the Apaches. The Pueblos were better off than these. When Mexico ceded her vast northern territory to the United States, the latter promised that they would honor agreements made between the Spanish or Mexican government and the Indians. The Pueblos lived in their own villages, the borders of which had been well defined for centuries. They therefore escaped the fate of the roaming tribes who were driven from their hunting grounds into reservations.

This did not save the Pueblos from severe problems from which they suffer to these days. The railroads came and the land filled with settlers. It was found that the Pueblos did not hold legal title to some land they had worked for generations. By 1890, every acre suitable for cattle grazing had been taken up by whites. They pushed back the Pueblos everywhere. Every square inch of desirable land near a river or brook was coveted by whites. By 1913, many white people squatted on Pueblo land to which the Indians held clear tittle. "The locusts have come," was the way the Pueblos put it.

Swarms of missionaries descended upon the Pueblo villages eager to save souls—for a Protestant god this time. They were new to the country and knew nothing about the Pueblos. They were puritan killjoys, forever shocked at the things Indians did. Their goal was "to make the Indians white." To achieve this, Indian children were taken forcibly from their homes to be put in faraway boarding schools where "civilization" was beaten into them with a strap. As late as 1906 Hopi children were not allowed to see their homes and parents for as long as ten years. The result was not what the missionaries hoped for. Out of the schools came young, bewildered people who could fit into neither the white nor the Pueblo world. Boys had been taught skills that might have been useful for office or factory workers, but useless in a Pueblo environment. Girls had been taught homemaking suitable for middle-class white city households.

Anglo missionaries of all denominations came imbued with a new, burning zeal to "civilize" and convert the Pueblos.

The missionaries began a campaign to stamp out the ancient native religion. For the Pueblos religion was inseparable from life. This meant that the missionaries attempted to stamp out the Indian. In this they were helped by the government, especially the all-powerful Bureau of Indian Affairs. It enacted a Religious Crimes Code under which Indians were jailed if they dared to practice their sacred rituals. The Commissioner of Indian Affairs called the Taos people "half-animals" when criticizing their rituals which did not fit in with his ideas of holiness. Freedom of religion was a "for whites only" thing.

The missionaries often destroyed the unity that governed the life of the Pueblos. Missionary influence created factions and tension between "modern" and "backward," Christian and "heathen," progressive and traditionalist Indians. At Laguna, a missionary couple destroyed two kivas. Fifty villagers then left to resettle at Isleta, taking many of the pueblo's sacred things with them. At Oraibi the people split into two hostile parties; half the population left and built themselves a new village. Hopi elders who objected to their being taken away to missionary school were jailed at Fort Defiance.

In nonreligious matters, too, the government knew what "was good for the Indian." The Pueblos knew their land as no white man ever could. Alfred Kidder, the famous archaeologist, who had studied them for a lifetime, spoke about: "the ability of the Pueblo Indian to support himself quite comfortably in the face of conditions which would stagger a white farmer." Yet white men now told the Indian what to plant and how to manage his herds. They tried to force upon the Pueblos the Allotment Act under which the ancestral, communal land was parceled out, bit by bit, to individual owners who could sell their acreage to outsiders if they wished. Hopi elders who resisted this act were imprisoned at Fort Wingate.

Government advisers introduced a number of domestic animals. This quickly led to overgrazing. As one expert said: "The introduction of livestock was the sole cause for the ruination of the Hopi country." Other experts came and told the Indians: "You have too much livestock, you must kill half of it off!" The result was disaster for many Indian families.

People think that the harm done to the Pueblos by white America is at matter of ancient history. People today generally sympa-

American missionaries worked hard to suppress native religion and ceremonies, especially the dances of the sacred clowns, or *koyemshi*. Possibly the aversion of missionaries had something to do with the outrageously hilarious way in which the clowns mimicked and made fun of the missionaries and other white spectators.

thize with Native Americans. Yet two races, two civilizations, two ways of life, are still at war. It has been a silent, undeclared war. Often the parties are not even aware that it is going on. Anglos and Pueblos have not faced each other in battle since the tragic day

The goal of Anglo education was to rear children away from home in boarding schools, to make them white inside and red outside. The result was children who were neither Pueblos nor Anglos, unable to relate to either of their two worlds.

when Taos was stormed in 1847. Yet, the destruction of Indian people, Indian land, and Indian culture goes on. "You once killed us with a gun," says one Hopi elder, "now you are killing us with a dollar bill."

The coal companies, the utilities, the oil and uranium interests, the natural gas people, land speculators, the highway lobby—all are trying to get their hands on the land of the Pueblos. Giant bulldozers strip the soil from the land of the Hopis and Navajos to get at the coal beneath. Giant power plants with 170-foot-high smokestacks spread a cloud of sulphurous smoke over the Four Corners area, a plume of smoke 200 miles long—the only man-made thing seen by the astronauts on their way to the moon.

"It is not always a big thing they are doing," says Santana Antonio of Acoma. "It can be something small, like cutting down our peach trees to make room for a bigger, wider, highway. They paid us for it, but can a tree be paid for, or an enchanted spot, or a way of life?"

"It all comes down to this," says an old man from Jemez. "You say you love us Indians. You'll do anything to right the old wrongs. But when it comes to a choice of running your TV sets and air-conditioners and other electric gadgets or not building huge power plants on Indian lands, then you will find our land expendable, as you put it. If it comes down to having no gas for your cars or having no Indians, then you will vote for having no Indians every time."

American society's insatiable greed for energy and land poses a serious threat to the Pueblos and all other Indians; but the greatest threat is, and has been for the past hundred years, that of being simply drowned in the sheer, overwhelming mass of numbers and technology.

From 1847 on the Pueblos were forced into closer and closer contact with whites. White administrators ruled their material and economic life. Teachers, doctors, archaeologists, anthropologists,

Americanization of the Southwest meant white teachers, social and health workers, as well as tourists, coming into the Pueblos.

traders, and swarms of tourists with clicking cameras overwhelmed their villages.

With the passage of time and an increase in the Pueblo population, from 10,000 in 1847 to 30,000 now, the strictly limited land base was, in many villages, not enough to feed all the people. Increasingly the Indians had to come out of their isolation in order to earn a living in the white world. Pueblo men and women could be seen at railroad stations and in the streets of Gallup, Albuquerque, or Santa Fe selling their silver and turquoise jewelry and their pottery. Men worked part time on farms and served in the armed forces; women worked in hotels, motels, shops, and hospitals.

Not only white people invaded the pueblos, but also white ideas and gadgets. By the end of the 1950s most pueblos had electricity and TV sets. Some resisted white technology as destructive to their way of life. In Taos the traditionalists ripped the electric wires from the walls of homes of returned veterans who wanted to have "modern houses." "Do it outside the village," they were told, "but not here." "TV is a dangerous thing," says Santana Antonio of Acoma. "Kids learn to watch it before they can talk. Then they learn English first and never learn their own tongue."

In 1924 the Pueblos were declared American citizens by an act of Congress. Citizenship was a reward for the Native Americans' faithful service in World War I. Congress thought they had done the Indians a great favor, but many Pueblos did not want this belated citizenship. "We are, and have always been, a nation of our own," they say, "long before you came." In 1971 Hopi elders refused to accept regular American passports and traveled to the environmental conference in Stockholm, Sweden, with their own handmade passports of deerskin. In the 1930s the administration did the Pueblos another favor by giving them constitutions and tribal governments patterned after white American institutions. This was supposed to bring democracy and a measure of self-government to the Pueblos. Unfortunately many Indians looked upon Anglo-imposed government as something alien which did not fit in with their way of doing things. They ignored it and refused to take part in its election, looking rather to the traditional caciques for leadership.

This, then, is the history of the people who have dwelt in the land

Hopi elders at the Stockholm Environmental Conference to speak on
behalf of mother earth. The Swedish people welcomed them with
bouquets of lily of the valley.

of canyon and mesa since the dawn of time—who have been in
turn the Basket Makers, the Anasazis, and now the Pueblos. Animals
became extinct, mountains eroded, climates changed, rivers left their
beds; the Pueblos just went on. We know their history, we must
now see them as people living among us, going about their daily
tasks, performing their rituals, pursuing their arts, getting born and

married and buried, always clinging to their ancient way of life. The Pueblos—it was expected, predicted, and wished for—should have long ago evaporated inside the melting pot, to become indistinguishable from other Americans. But this did not happen. Pointing to one of the gigantic new power stations with its bewildering maze of pipes and twisted steel, a white-haired Hopi elder said: "Our children's children will still be praying in their kivas long after all this mess is gone."

A wall of guardians protects the church and cemetery of Acoma.

# 9 ▪ INVISIBLE WALLS

The Anglo pays a man a compliment by calling him a "rugged individualist." He prides himself on standing on his own two feet, on making it on his own, on doing *his* thing, on showing qualities of leadership, on competing successfully in the marketplace, on being able to "sell himself," on acquiring status, on keeping up with the Joneses.

"White men live right next door to us now," said an old man from Jemez, "but in our heads we are a world apart. We just think differently." The Pueblo is the opposite of an individualist. He does not "do *his* thing," he thinks only as one of a group. His morality is based on the common good. The loneliness of the white man stuck away in a housing project where all live as strangers, tucked away in their individual cubicles, near to but totally separated from one another, each nuclear family pursuing its own interests, is utterly beyond the Pueblo's understanding.

He exists only as part of a group—his clan, his kiva, his village—a living link between those who have come before him and those who are still to come. A reed, by itself, can be broken by a child; but many reeds, tied together in a bundle, are unbreakable. Thus, each has the strength of many. A man does not work a field just to fill his own belly, but according to a plan laid down by his gods at the beginning of time. If he neglects his field it can be taken from him to be given to another because it is not really *his* field,

In some pueblos time seems to stand still. Traditional Pueblo people are not fond of change, yet it creeps in. For example, a new modern adobe house springing up among centuries-old buildings at Acoma.

but the pueblo's. People of a clan come together out of habit to build a house or cut wheat. The sheep owner limits his herd to a size compatible with the amount of communal pasture and water alloted to him. The Pueblo cannot and will not pray alone for his own personal gain. Not even the village chief, the priest, the holy man prays except within the context of well-established rituals which benefit all. The chief priest plants prayer sticks only when he is supposed to, and never for himself.

This sense of unity finds expression in the Pueblo's religion. He knows no personalized god created after his own image, but knows the spirit embodied in a cloud, in an animal, or in a pebble. He knows no separation from his gods. He prays to them: "We shall be one person." During a Kachina dance, god and man become one. Even his town comes out of Mother Earth, an extension of the soil, forever crumbling back into it, and forever renewed with a few handfuls of native mud.

All are part of one another. Almost a century ago Frank H. Cushing, a student of Zuñi culture, wrote about one pueblo: "One remarkable feature of the Zuñi had impressed me—the well-regulated life they lead. At one season they are all absorbed in harvesting, at another, in the sacred obligations; now games led the way." In this way life experience is common to all, shared at the same time in the same way. Cushing also wrote that "paupers and drones are unknown among them" meaning that within a village all were taken care of and all did their part. The Pueblo Indian, the same writer said, "has a natural serenity that the white man can never attain." And no wonder!

There is no pressure to become wealthy, to get ahead, to acquire fame, to be a leader. There are no suicides among the Pueblo, no murders, no violence, no locked doors, no reasons to be uptight. There is an almost total lack of envy. Here are people who have no wish to be anything but what they are—*Pueblo Indians.*

Never left out in the cold, always a part of a larger whole, the Pueblo has a sense of security unknown even to other Indian tribes who do not have a similar communal structure to fall back on. For this reason there is little drunkenness in a pueblo compared to

Dancing the old dances and performing the ancient ceremonies is one way for the Pueblo to retain their identity. This was the case throughout the 19th century and it is the case today.

Plains reservations or Indian urban ghettoes. While many members of other tribes have found aid and comfort in the peyote religion, it has made little headway inside Pueblo villages. They see no need for mystical visions of a better world, nor do they seek power by self-torture or flesh-offerings as do some Plains Indians. They do not wish to escape the bounds of their own body and senses through pain, fasting, visions, or alcohol. They accept the world—*their world*—joyfully, "because it has always been there and has always helped and sustained us."

Of course, the Pueblo is holding on to his world by trying to ignore the white world as much as possible, even in some cases by shutting it out of his mind altogether. That is not easy to do and can even be dangerous to his survival. Surrounded on all sides by insecurity, the Pueblo protects his security by walls of age-old traditions. The pueblos are thus so many besieged fortresses. Once the walls are breached, the structure of communal life crumbles. The village splits into factions of "conservatives" and "progressives," of those who want to remain what they have always been and those who want to adopt the white people's ways.

If the "progressives" win, the essential "Puebloness" of the village will be destroyed, the fabric which holds everything together will be ripped apart. The traditionalists will then go away to settle elsewhere, taking the pueblo's sacred things with them. The traditionalists gone, the old stories and ceremonials will be soon forgotten by the people. And what they forget or discard will be lost forever, because some things are not and should not be written down.

The pueblo will then become a living ghost. Dances will still be performed, but for show only. What does it matter if a man or woman wears old tennis shoes during a corn dance instead of leggings or moccasins? What does it matter if a hairdo is wrong or a mask is missing? The dance will have lost its meaning anyhow. The village will still be there. It will still look picturesque. The tourists will still come and be welcome to take pictures—for a fee. Soon the "atmosphere" will be gone, too, the old houses replaced by ugly little adobes with screen doors and TV antennas. Soon the land developers will come and the energy boys will wave their money around and be listened to. The village will linger on, maybe for a long time, but it will be just a name on a map. It will have ceased to be a pueblo.

In a few villages this has happened. They stand as a grim warn-

To see a Pueblo dance is an unforgettable experience. Most dances are sacred religious ceremonies, prayers for rain and a good harvest. You are welcome to watch, provided you follow the rules laid down for visitors.

ing to others. In some very rare cases, the people have second thoughts. The traditionalists reassert themselves. The exiles lay the basis for existence elsewhere. Some of the old ways and rituals miraculously survive, even make a comeback. But usually the process, once started, is irreversible. So closely are the people interwoven and dependent upon one another to uphold the old ways, that once their unity is broken and their defenses breached, there is little they can do to resist what then becomes inevitable.

So, to preserve their identity and the continuity of their lives the

Pueblos have put up invisible walls to guard them from the enemy. The enemy is you and I, the visitor, the casual tourist with his ever-ready camera who cannot understand why he should not photograph a kiva which, after all, has been photographed before. The well-meaning schoolteacher trying to instill a sense of competition in her Indian pupils to "prepare them for life" in space-age America. The equally well-meaning official from the Bureau of Land Management or some other government agency with the man from the coal or utility in tow. Doesn't he bring jobs and dollars? And always the anthropologist with his notebook and tape recorder asking a hundred questions.

The Pueblos and the surrounding and intruding Anglos, even the well-meaning, knowledgeable ones, are all soldiers in a silent but very real fight for the Indian's survival *as Pueblos*, not just as slightly darker skinned *ex-Pueblo* motel waitresses or curio sellers. The Pueblo knows he is a soldier on an invisible firing line. The Anglo, more often than not, is unaware of his role. So, when you are forbidden to take a picture of a gorgeous dance you are dying to project on the screen for your friends back home, don't be mad. If you are shooed away from a ritual you are not meant to see, if the welcome mat is not out for you, don't be insulted. The Pueblos, by nature, are friendly and hospitable.

Many years ago, Frank Cushing came to Zuñi uninvited. He just walked in and settled down for months in a house the owners of which he did not know. He forced his way into rituals though his presence was a sacrilege. He took notes and made sketches of secret rites, and when the Indians tried to take them away from him he waved a sharp knife in their faces. He thought that his scientific quest for knowledge was sufficient excuse for his behavior, yet his unwilling Zuñi hosts sheltered and fed him, giving him water when he was thirsty, cooking for him when he was hungry, covering him with blankets when he was cold.

A rude, brash, domineering intruder, this man considered himself the Zuñis' friend. Maybe we should not be too hard on him, because his behavior reflected the attitude of his time—the late nineteenth and early twentieth centuries—when whites thought themselves superior to other people, when a man was considered civilized if his home had a flush toilet. Fortunately, those days are over. If a Pueblo turns you away, do not be angry at him. He is trying to preserve an ancient heritage—for you as well as for himself. And do not rejoice over the friendly, grinning "apple" who would let you take a picture on the sly and who would sell you the secrets of his people for a dollar. The chances are he doesn't know any secrets anyway.

The Pueblos' fight to remain themselves is a hard one. It requires them to live in two worlds at once, to live—as the psychologists say—as a "split-personality," because even the most conservative villages cannot keep Anglos, and Anglo ways, out altogether. It has to deal with them on one level, while continuing as it has always been on another. Over fifty years ago a discerning and sympathetic writer, Charles Lummis, clearly saw the nature of the Indians' silent fight for survival. The Pueblo, he said, "as an Indian is a paradox; as a man, he is unique. He enjoys two religions, irreconcilable yet reconciled, two sets of laws—American, and his own, two languages and two names—one given him during the sacrament of Christian baptism—while the other, whereby he goes among his own, was sealed upon his infant lips with the spittle of an Indian godfather at a pagan feast."

The first of the Pueblos' defense is their inborn conservatism. As one writer put it: "They set their faces like flint against all innovation." Things are "because they have been always so." Pueblos are conservative because they have something of value to conserve, to hold on to. They like to keep the outside away for as long and as far as possible.

Christianity and the Kachina cult exist side by side. Pueblo children going to a Catholic mass.

As Lummis noted in his book   *Mesa, Canyon and Pueblo*:

When we find a spot of beauty or of wonder, our first thought is to make it "accessible" so that everyone can get to it without any trouble greater than that of paying his fare and his accommodation. The commercial spirit is first and foremost. With the Indian, on the other hand, his precise desire was to have such a spot that everybody could *not* get to it, so that it would be safe for those to whom it belonged, and who were willing to take the trouble to get there.

There should not even be boundary marks around a village; they are a white invention, disliked by the supernaturals. Wherever possible, one should do without Anglo gadgets. In some places the introduction of electric lights and plumbing are forbidden within the old, central pueblo. Most have some offshoots, little settlements in which much of the secular life, the farming, and the sheepherding is done. Electric light might be all right there, at a safe distance from the kivas, but not for the sacred place.

Up to a few years ago, Taos men were still fined five dollars if they wore American Levi's unless they removed the seat and wrapped some blanket around their hips as a sort of breechcloth. Men were told to wear their white cotton wraparounds and to keep their hair braided. In the late 1960s the herald from the housetops called out to Taos women not to go to the white people's hospital to give birth, but to have their babies at home where nature would take care of them as she had for a thousand years before.

All these measures are not the crazy whims of a few crotchety old men. They are part of the walls defending the Pueblo way of life. We should wish the old men well, because without their stubbornness, maintained over almost five hundred years of white dominance, there would be no pueblos now. The extent of the Pueblos' conservatism varies from village to village. It is strong among the Hopis and at Santo Domingo, almost nonexistent at Laguna, weakening at Cochiti. In any villages an uneasy coexistence prevails between the old and the new. A few years ago at Zuñi, I saw a good example of this. In the old plaza an unbelievably beautiful masked dance was performed. My family was invited to come inside a house on the plaza to have corn and bread. From inside one of its rooms we could see the dancers in their costumes and hear the beat of the drum. But in the same room, some teen-agers were watching John Wayne fighting Apaches with a great banging away of gunfire, and the commercial was telling them that nine out of ten doctors preferred this and that for post-nasal drip. Watching the idiot box, they were oblivious to the beauty and mystery unfolding in the ancient plaza. The sacred rites were still performed, but the enemy had opened

Since the coming of strip mining, whites are no longer always welcome at Hopi Snake Dances.

a crack in the door and put his foot in it. The Zuñis were confident they could handle him. Maybe so, but it will not be easy.

The second wall protecting the Pueblos is secrecy. This wall is not weakening, it is actually getting stronger. A sacred dance, a ritual, a song inside a kiva represent a mystical power used for the good of the people. Power talked about is power lost. Sacred power captured in a picture is power taken away. A medicine bundle in a museum glass case is power rendered useless.

There are things the old people know, but don't talk about—at least not to the outsider. Like their secret Indian names, or the real name of their village. In the 1880s and '90s white anthropologists forced their way into kivas, desecrating them while the Indians stood by helpless and embarrassed, not knowing what to do. Before World War I many rituals, such as the Hopi Snake Dance, were still photographed. But the Indians found out about cameras, and heard white spectators describe their ceremonies as barbarous and obscene. So photography of rituals was forbidden. Anybody attempting to take pictures of them now is liable to have his camera smashed, and his tape recorder, too.

Up to a year or two ago whites were welcome to watch the sacred dances—without cameras, notebooks, and recording devices. But then came the strip miners and the land speculators and "developers." Some Pueblos felt that the presence of so many white curiosity seekers weakened their ceremonies so that they could no longer protect the people from these new, threatening encroachments. So whites are no longer always welcome to see the Snake Dance. Even the fake snake and rain dances put on for tourists only at Gallup, Flagstaff, and Prescott are now subject to angry Indian demonstrations. They may be fake, but they are aping a genuine ritual, making a mockery of it. The wall of secrecy gets stronger every year.

The third invisible wall is the wall of self-government. The Pueblos are in fact tiny nations, similar in a way to the ancient city-states of Greece. Their governments are theocratic, that is, the rulers, if one can call them that, are priests who conduct the pueblo's business according to customs handed down to the people through the ages by the Trues, the deities. There is no "separation of church and state."

Charles Lummis said: "The Pueblo Indians have a complete government of their own, each village being an independent and full-fledged republic, with a great body of sound and sensible laws, and with perfectly competent machinery to enforce them and to administer justice."

At the head of the Pueblo government stands the cacique. The name was imported by the Spaniards. It is supposed to be a word used by early Caribbean Indians meaning "chief." It is not a Pueblo word. The Hopi call such a man *kikmongwi.* The Zuñi call him *pekwin,* the Keresan-speaking villages *traikatse* or *tiamuny.* He always serves for life. His office is hereditary, handed down through his mother's bloodline. The cacique is a priest; he has the final authority over sacred and profane matters. If he fails in his task he can be removed from office by the war chief and the council of elders, but this almost never happens. In some places there are two caciques—a summer chief and a winter chief.

The cacique holds himself a little apart from humdrum, everyday affairs; he concentrates on spiritual things. He never takes part in quarrels; he will not even hear or see them. One does not use rough language within his earshot. He never shows anger. Nothing about which there is not unanimous agreement is brought to his attention. He determines the best times to plant and harvest according to the solstices, regulates the village calendar, and fixes dates for dances and ceremonies. He counsels but does not command. He is the very opposite of a dictator.

The cacique is helped by two, sometimes three warchiefs. In the old days they commanded the warriors in battle, but for a long time now they have performed other tasks. They are much concerned with the religious life of the village. They help with the ceremonies. They act like secretaries of state busying themselves with the "foreign affairs" of their little pueblo state.

An important part of this traditional government is a council of elders. They are wise and strong. The people who make up a traditional pueblo's government are the men "who know how." Cushing said that in the Zuñi language there are five words meaning "to know." *First,* there is knowledge of the land, of places, rivers and mountains. *Second,* there is the knowledge of people, of friends, of

At Acoma men pray and sing before the *ḳisi,* a hut made of branches and leaves. This picture was taken in the 1890s.

animals, and of things. *Third,* there is the knowledge to act, to speak, and to think. *Fourth,* there is the knowledge gained by understanding, by discerning, by experience, and by having lived long. *Fifth,* there is the knowledge of the beyond, the flash of insight, knowledge that cannot be seen but can be felt, knowledge of the unknowable. A good, wise, older man should have the first four knowledges; but a cacique, a war chief and a medicine man should also have the fifth.

Pueblos were and are peaceful and nonviolent. Men who killed an enemy in battle, even in self-defense, were unpure for many months. At Zuñi, they were not allowed to sleep with their wives for over a year. No matter how hard men quarreled, they never came to blows. Murders within a village were unheard of. Even in punishing evildoers violence was avoided. Years ago, a drunken drifter shot an Isleta woman. He was tracked down by men with rifles. He forted up behind boulders and sniped at his pursuers. But the story had no John Wayne ending. There was no shoot-out. The Pueblos patiently and deftly stunned the offender with thrown rocks until he surrendered.

This attitude is reflected in the Pueblo government which strives

The same scene now. Some things do not change.

for two things above all: harmony and unanimity. Before a council meeting men might pray: "Let us move evenly together." They will say: "We are all in one nest." Therefore there are no factions, no loyal opposition. A party struggle, the Indians think, could easily finish their village. Frank Cushing once had a disagreement about something or other with the old Zuñi man in whose house he lived. As soon as Cushing got angry and raised his voice, the old man got up to leave the room. "Where are you going, my father?" Cushing asked. "It grieves me to see my son show his anger," said the old man and left.

Important tribal matters are thrashed out until everybody agrees upon one solution. This can take up much time. But impatience and haste are Anglo, not Pueblo, diseases. In the end, all will agree upon what has to be done.

In this kind of traditional government there are no office-seekers and no salaries, no campaigning, no back-slapping, no electioneering, no deals. A pushy, self-seeking person is a rarity. He is considered abnormal. Rather, the Pueblo shuns office. This is no wonder. Holding office for a Pueblo means working hard without any pay, taking care of the people's business while neglecting one's own. It means being unable to tend one's own fields or earn money on some outside job. There are not even the trappings of power which so delight the white officeholder. The position of cacique is honored, but not the person who holds it. The man is not treated with more respect or deference than anybody else in the village. His house is no better than all the other houses. A cacique may be a raggedy-looking, old man whose pants are mended, and whose shirt is without buttons. The clothes do not matter, but what is inside does.

A man has to be persuaded to accept office. In one pueblo, a man whom his fellow villagers chose to be war chief refused the honor and had to be kept in jail until he changed his mind. At Isleta, ac-

Performing Pueblo ceremonies to attract tourist dollars is coming under increased criticism by Indian traditionalists.

cording to Lummis, a reluctant candidate for governor was set astride a fence post, his legs tied beneath him, until he gave in and consented to serve. The people learn about their government's decisions from the town crier "who with a long, musical call, proclaims the cacique's orders." One early author described "the distant erect figure of the herald against a twilight sky, a serape thrown gracefully over his shoulders like a Roman toga."

We have seen that the Pueblo Indian has to live in two different worlds. That is especially true when it comes to his tribal government. Side by side with the cacique, his war chiefs, and his group of elders exists an altogether different kind of administration: the

In many pueblos, such as in Taos, the herald, or town crier, still relays
messages from the caciques to the people.

governor, lieutenant governor, and officially elected tribal council.
This parallel administration is imposed on the Pueblos and other
tribes and reservations by the U.S. government. It is patterned after
the white "Wa-sin-to-na" administration.

If the Pueblo lives in harmony and unity, the governor is often
chosen by the cacique and the elders and the following election is
just a show of common consent on the part of the villagers. In that
case the governor fulfills an important function. He serves as a buffer
between the traditional government and the outside world. The
cacique is a spiritual leader. He does not want to soil his mind and
hands with the distasteful business of dealing with the Anglo of-

ficials who are often not even aware of his existence. They do not know the traditional Pueblo government. They ignore it as it ignores them. In many cases the governor with his Washington-type administration is the only government the whites know.

The governor has the appearance, but not the substance, of power. He follows the orders of a hidden government above him. But he carries the official cane of office topped by a silver knob given to Pueblo governors a long time ago by President Lincoln. The governor has much to do. He deals with tourists, roadbuilders, anthropologists, state officials, the men from Health, Education, and Welfare, people from the Bureau of Indian Affairs.

It sometimes happens that the governor and his men have dealt so closely and for so long with the outside world that they begin to think and act like whites. This can turn them into tools of the white government, or of other ouside interests. They may think that they are doing a good job for the people. The white way, they say, is better, more advanced. "Let's make some money selling the coal underneath our soil. We don't need it, but we sure need the dollars which can buy so many things for us who are so poor. Let's get some industry in here, and dams, and a resort area for well-heeled white customers. Think of the jobs this will bring, of the progress, of the better living standard."

If that happens, then the old-style and the new-style governments will fight, and the pueblo will be in deep trouble. The Indians cannot do much to prevent such a situation because the elective white government has been forced upon them from Washington, "to bring enlightenment and democracy to the untutored Indians."

As if two governments were not enough, the Pueblos have to contend with a third one—the all-powerful Bureau of Indian Affairs which holds the purse strings and runs the schools and hospitals, the utilities, the roads, and the finances—a monster of innumerable functions and great resources which is forever trying to regulate the

Indians' lives. The Bureau has immense power to benefit or harm the Pueblos. In the opinion of a good many Indians, especially the young activists, harm by far outweighs benefit.

If all goes well, as it does in the majority of the pueblos, the traditional hidden government of the caciques fulfills its function as the third barrier to outside encroachment. A fourth and last invisible wall of protection is the Pueblos' ancient religion. It comprises all the other walls because there is no distinction between religion and secular things. All are one. All aspects of the Indians' government and daily existence are but part of their faith. Politics and dances, work and games, irrigation or planting, birth and marriage and death—all are an integral part of Pueblo religion. As one early writer put it: "If we would pick the threads of religion from the warp and woof of Hopi life, there apparently would not be much left." The old Indian religion, going back to the ancient Anasazis and the Basket Makers, is the Pueblos' shield and hope. And it is getting stronger.

If a civilization is in balance; if all its various parts are a harmonious One; if governors and governed are the same; if no part of human activity overshadows another; if man and his surroundings move in natural rhythm with one another; if art, religion, and government are all manifestations of the same great plan—then that civilization will happily stand the test of time in spite of all misfortunes. "Let our invisible walls stand," say the Pueblos.

# 10 ▪ BIRTH, LIFE, AND DEATH

*May you always live without sickness,*
*May you have good corn and all good things,*
*May you travel the Sun Trail to old age,*
*And pass away in sleep without pain.*

PRAYER AT A BABY'S NAMING CEREMONY

The birth of a Pueblo child is a joyous, longed-for event. Long before a baby is born, the parents observe many rules, and try to behave in a way that will make the birth easy and bring forth a healthy child. Mostly, this is a matter of *not* doing certain things. The mother-to-be wears her hair loose and makes sure that there are no knots in her clothing, or anywhere around her person, because this would "tie up" the baby and render the birth-giving difficult. For the same reason, she does not start to go out of the house and then hesitate and go back, or start out on a walk and then return for something or other without finishing her errand. She does not let other persons walk in front of her or hold other people's babies in her lap. All these things could make the birth long and painful.

A woman is also careful not to look at a snake, or even the ceremonial image of a snake, for that could turn the baby into a water serpent which will twist itself around the wrong way inside its mother so that, instead of emerging head first, it might come into the world feet first, which would be dangerous. And, of course, the mother-to-be avoids looking at anything deformed or ugly. In some villages, an expectant mother is told not to go to the movies, otherwise her child might be born twitchy and lacking in good sense, acting silly like the figures on the screen.

The father also takes care not to do anything that could hurt the unborn child, such as tying the neck of his horse, or burro, too tightly

A classic 19th-century photograph of a Pueblo mother and her baby, called *A Hopi Madonna.*

to a fence post, because this could result in the baby being strangled by its own navel cord. Above all, the father is not cruel to living creatures lest, by doing such a bad thing, he might harm his own child. A man who, without meaning to do so, crushed a puppy's hind leg with a heavy load, saw his baby born with a deformed foot.

There are so many things one should *not* do that it is hard to keep track of them. On the other hand, there are a few things one *should* do. The mother, for instance, should keep herself busy and active with daily chores until the last moment so as to be slim and in good shape when her hour arrives. Among the Hopi, a man should bring his wife some meat from a weasel, and rub her body with the fur of this swift and agile animal. This will bring the baby into the world with the same speed and ease as that with which a weasel emerges from its burrow.

Many Pueblo babies are born at home, not in a hospital. An older, experienced relative, often the grandmother or aunt, acts as the mid-wife, or "childbirth woman." A medicine man might also be called to help. At Isleta, for instance, he will rub the mother's back with a magic stone to "unloosen" her. In some villages, he might touch the woman's body with a badger's paw "because the badger digs her-self out quickly, and just as quickly the paw will bring about an easy birth." Sometimes the mother is given the picture of a saint to hold, the kind of saint who is known to protect women in childbirth.

The birth takes place on a specially prepared pile of sand, some-times warmed with stones; in some places on an animal skin. If the baby is a boy, the navel cord is cut with a sharp arrowhead, which will make him into a good hunter. The newborn child is washed gently in warm water and sprinkled with juniper ashes. "These will keep the baby from becoming too hairy," say the Hopis and Zuñis. In many villages, mother and child are also purified by having their heads washed in yucca suds.

Four marks of cornmeal are made by the grandmother on the four walls of the room in which the baby is born. A little sacred cornmeal is placed on the baby's lips. It is then wrapped in a cotton blanket and swaddled in its cradle board, in which it will spend most of its time during the first six months—sometimes longer. A Pueblo woman told me: "The cradle board teaches the baby our way, to be contained, stay put. It is the baby's pueblo."

After giving birth, the mother and her newborn are kept in the house, away from all sunlight, for anywhere from four to twenty days, depending on the village. During this time a fire is kept going to keep evil spirits away. The mother is also given good, strong medi-cine in the form of juniper tea. At the end of this period of confinement the baby is presented to the sun and given its name. At Acoma this happens on the fourth day after the baby's birth, early in the morning, before sunrise. A medicine man with his wife will come to the parents' house. He will make a sand painting on the floor of one of the rooms. It will be the design of a turtle or a horned toad which will bring the baby luck and long life. "The turtle heart," say some Indians, "keeps on beating long after the turtle is dead." Turtles and lizards have the power to make the child grow up and become very old. A belief in this power is common to many tribes, not only to some of the Pueblo people. A turtle design might be used also in a prayer for rain, because "this is an animal which likes the water."

While the medicine man makes his sand painting, his wife is bathing the mother and baby. The medicine man then sings over the child to the sound of a gourd rattle. He asks the parents whether they have chosen a name for their baby. If they have not, he himself will name the little one. The blackness of the night has given way to a gray dawn. It is time to go to the eastern edge of the high mesa. As the red, glowing ball of the sun rises over the edge of the high cliff, the medicine man's wife holds up the baby—"letting it be kissed by the sun." Her husband inhales deeply, then blows at the baby, giving him the breath of life. He solemnly pronounces the baby's name, his Indian name, not to be revealed to strangers. The medicine man's wife, followed by her husband, then carries the baby to the house where the parents are waiting. The medicine man is praying, pronouncing the baby's name again: "Here he comes, this is his home, may he have long life, all manner of crops, fruit, and game. He is coming." The parents answer joyfully, "Let him come in," and receive their baby. Breakfast is then prepared. Steam from the food is fanned toward the sand painting with eagle plumes, and a morsel of food is placed beside the turtle's head—a meal for its spirit. The medicine man ties an ear of sacred corn to the cradle board "on the side where the baby's heart is, so that it may never want." The medicine man then sweeps up the sand painting and leaves with his wife. The naming ceremony is over.

Among the Hopi, it is on the twentieth day that the baby is presented to the Sun Father. Here it is not a medicine man, but usually the grandmother on the father's side who plays the main role. Here, too, mother and baby are washed in yucca suds. A line of cornmeal is sprinkled from the cradle to the door—the Hopi road of life. Relatives of both parents crowd the house. Outside the father is eagerly watching for the first ray of sunlight, and the moment it appears he gives the signal. At once the godmother, followed by the mother, carries the baby to the mesa's edge, lifting up the little one to the bright-shining godhead, saying prayers, touching the baby's lips

Grandmothers play a very important role in the children's upbringing.

with cornmeal. Both women also sprinkle cornmeal toward the sun, calling out to the sun god the baby's name so that he might know and acknowledge it. The child is also blessed with ears of corn. Afterward, all eat piki, the native bread, boiled meat, and many other delicacies.

From the moment of its birth a Pueblo child is surrounded by relatives, ceremonial fathers and mothers, who all take a great interest in its welfare and play an important role in its life. This emphasizes that, among the Pueblos, the basis of society is not the family but the clan—a much wider circle of close human relationships.

The name given a child when it is "shown to the sun" is its first, Indian name, sometimes more than one. In many pueblos, there will be a christening later in the Catholic church, during which the child will receive its white name. In some villages a Spanish name given to a family many generations ago by a Spanish padre is used. The child usually will bear its mother's family name because descent is traced from the mother, not from the father, as is the case among white Americans. This is the name by which the child will be known to the outside world. From the earliest days of its life, the child will be one of two worlds and two beliefs, trying to exist in harmony with both.

In a few pueblos little of the old ceremonies remains. People no longer bother to observe the many symbolic parts of a rite, such as the baby's name-giving ritual which, among traditional tribes, is much more complex than described here. But if the child is born in a family that holds to the old ways, then it will be brought up from the first moment as much as that is possible today, to act and live as its grandfathers and grandmothers of old; or, as a Laguna missionary described it: "The newborn babe is hushed to sleep with custom song, gets custom medicine, and grows up in the very bosom of religious custom."

The baby spends the first months of its life in the cradle board.

Cradleboards were used by all southwestern tribes to tote babies around. White mothers, too, are now discovering the practicality of similar devices.

How long often depends on the child. If the baby is very restless, kicks much, or yells much, it might be taken out of its cradle board during the day after six months. A quiet and contented baby, on the other hand, might spend a whole year in it, but after that time all babies are out of the cradle board and busy learning to walk.

Indians have been using cradle boards for a long time. They have been found in the ancient ruins of the Anasazi. Many human skulls in prehistoric graves are flattened at the back—a sure sign of the use of cradle boards. Even when you look at Pueblo people today, you will often notice that the back of their heads is a little flatter and straighter than that of white Americans. The Pueblo's head is shaped while it is still soft, resting against the wooden back of the cradle board for long periods of time.

Cradle boards, called *ta-qui-ru,* protect the baby's body. They are comfortable, sanitary, and very practical. With the baby inside they can be leaned against the wall, laid flat on a table, or suspended by two ropes from the ceiling like a hammock. They can be slung over the mother's back making it easy to carry the baby around. Their hood of willow twigs, or round wooden headband, is handy to hold away from the baby's face, a blanket against the cold, or a screen against the flies. At Acoma cradle boards were made of trees struck by lightning which were supposed to have a protective charm. Among Zuñis cradle boards were given a "heart"—a small piece of turquoise.

In the old days, Pueblo mothers used cedar bark instead of diapers. Nowadays, cedar bark is out and Pampers are in. Cradle boards are so practical that many of their features have been incorporated in gadgets making it possible for modern white mothers to carry their baby, Indian fashion, wherever they go.

As everywhere else in the world, Pueblo women like to sing to their little ones. Here is one of their lullabies:

> *Go to sleep*
> *Little sleepy bird,*
> *Go to sleep,*
> *Or someone will take you away,*
> *So you better go to sleep*
> *Little bird.*

Clothing a child was no problem. Children used to run around naked as nature made them, up to the age of ten, in what one nineteenth-century writer called "the chaste indecency of childhood." Missionaries and white officials did not like this and lectured the Indians unceasingly about the shamefulness of nudity, even in small children. The Indians gave in and began clothing their little ones. From about 1915 on, they were dressed like all other children.

A Hopi family in the 1880s. As you see, clothing the smaller children was no great problem then.

Pueblo parents are permissive. Once children have learned to walk, they come and go as they please. They do not have to be on time for regular meals, though they will usually show up for them. They sleep whenever they are drowsy and can, if they want to, spend a night with friends or relatives. A pueblo is a very safe place for a child to roam about, and parents do not have to worry all the time about what the youngsters are doing, as they would in a big city. Children are not overprotected. A small girl will not be told over and over again: "Don't climb that chair, table, or rock." She might slip and fall, but that is one way to learn. A little boy's mother might warn him that the stove is hot, but if he ignores her and touches it, well, then he finds out what "hot" means.

*(Left)* Children at an early age take part in the ceremonies and fiestas of their people. This young girl from Jemez is helped by her mother to be dressed for a traditional dance.

*(Right)* These young boys are participating in an all-Indian powwow, showing off their skills to the outside world.

Children are taught to respect old people; not to wander into a kiva; not to fight, injure, or make fun of others; not to hurt animals. Nobody tells them not to say any "bad words" because these simply do not occur in the Indian language. Boys and girls are rarely punished, seldom yelled at, and almost never beaten. They may, however, be teased or shamed into good behavior. If that does not help, they might be scared into it by being told that a bogeyman, monster, or evil spirit will come and take them away. This generally does the trick, though many white parents would frown upon this method.

A child is taught things as soon as he or she is able to utter words and understand them. As far as the Pueblos are concerned, theirs is

a "scholarship of the senses"—learning by seeing, listening, and touching. A child would not be taught, but shown. From early age, boys and girls take an active part in all the activities of their family and village. A boy watches his father ride a horse or burro and imitates him until he has learned how. Girls watch their aunts and mothers making pottery and they too learn by "doing it." Children begin early to help with the grownup's chores. The environment, also, is a good teacher. Pueblo children grow up as a part of their surroundings as nature unfolds her secrets to them. Thus their senses are sharpened in a way that is beyond the city dweller's understanding.

As in the old days, the children learn the legends of their people from the storytellers.

One of my old Pueblo friends can recognize every footpath and goat trail within a hundred miles of her village, and knows exactly where it leads to, even if she has not seen it for ten or twenty years. On a camping trip, on a moonless, starless night, she has an unfailing sense of direction, saying, "There is north, and there is south," without ever being wrong. Yet, in a strange city, among skyscrapers, she will get lost within a few blocks. Most important, boys and girls are being prepared for adulthood, for the age-old tasks they will have to perform when they grow up, and which they in turn will teach to their children.

In his autobiography, *Sun Chief,* Don Talayeswa, a Hopi elder, described the essence of Pueblo education:

Learning to work was like play. We children tagged around with our elders and copied what they did. We followed our fathers to the fields and helped plant and weed. The old men took us for walks and taught us the use of plants. . . . We joined the women in gathering rabbitweed for baskets, and went with them to dig clay for pots. We watched the fields to drive out the birds and rodents, helped pick peaches to dry in the sun. . . . All the old people said that it was a disgrace to be idle and that a lazy boy should be whipped.

This learning through helping usually starts at age six or seven. Boys learn to haul wood, to hunt, to watch the sheep, or to guard the horses. In the old days they also learned to weave, because this is men's work. Today, weaving is a dying art.

Young girls fetch water for drinking and cooking in large pots called *ollas,* which they learn to carry gracefully on their heads leaving their hands free to climb up and down ladders or stairs to the waterhole. They do this because some Pueblo families do not have tap water or indoor plumbing. Girls learn to cook, to make pottery, to keep the house clean. Formerly young girls spent three hours a day grinding corn on the *metate,* which was hard work, even though a boy might play a flute for them to make their labor easier. Nowadays there is much less grinding to do, because more and more flour is bought at the store. One main task for a girl is to help take care of baby. Often one can see a quite small girl toting a much too big, fat baby on her back, staggering under the load, but with a big smile on her face.

Though some tasks are traditionally performed by men, and others by women, it will please those who feel strongly about women's rights that equality between the sexes was practiced by the Pueblos long before white people thought of it. Pueblo boys and men are not thought "unmanly" if they tote babies around or take care of them. Nor are they embarrassed to be seen weaving a blanket, darning their socks, or repairing their clothing. Some things are done by both men and women, such as the building and repair of houses, or the making of fine jewelry. At Zuñi, at all times, children are taught "to show a shining face, even when unhappy, and to listen to old people, who do not lie, and who know things."

But, of course, there is the matter of living in two worlds. Pueblo children, while learning the way of their people, must also learn the way of white America. Pueblo children go to school where the teachers are mostly white, and where they learn much the same things as are taught elsewhere throughout the country.

When schooling for Indians was started, shortly before the turn of the century, policemen often had to come and drag the children away to school by force. In many pueblos the people wanted to have nothing to do with whites and especially with white schools. They feared schools would destroy their culture and ancient beliefs. They were right to be fearful. The schools were run mostly by missionaries who tried to take the children away from the influence of their parents and relatives, educating them to be "like white people." In order to isolate the children from their former way of life, they were often taken to faraway boarding schools and sometimes did not see their villages or families for years. Great efforts were made to teach them English and "Anglo ways," to make them forget their own language and traditions. Being taken to school was therefore an occasion for tears, for hiding, and for running away.

Luckily, schools have changed since then and are happier places today. Great progress has been made lately to make teaching more relevant to Pueblo children. Some textbooks are made especially for them. Instead of the usual "See Spot run" book showing white

Among the Pueblos, weaving has always been a man's task. Here a Hopi is spinning wool for use in making sashes and blankets. The art of weaving has died out in many pueblos.

children in a city situation, newer books have stories and pictures of Indian children tending lambs or riding horses. Schools no longer try to force an alien culture upon their pupils, but teach Indian values. At the same time, they aim to educate children so that later they will be able to live in the outside world if they so desire.

Often the textbooks are more geared to white, big-city pupils and are not relevant to Pueblo children's lives.

Parents now take an active interest in the schools, and the number of Indian teachers is increasing.

Some problems remain. A white Acoma teacher said: "These children are wonderful, well behaved, bright and gifted, but they refuse to compete. They have no urge to get ahead, if that means getting ahead of another child. Sometimes they know perfectly well the answer to a question, but are too shy to give it, because they don't want to show up a classmate. Often I feel that they think it is cruel to show that they know more than another child, but in order to get ahead one must compete. I would like them to go on to college, but most of them are content to stay here raising sheep, doing what

To make school more relevant to Indian life, teachers in Albuquerque
have created paintings showing traditional Pueblo ways.

their fathers have done before them. I would like them to become
doctors, engineers, maybe forest rangers. There's not enough progress." From her point of view, the teacher may be right; but most
Pueblos do not think that "getting ahead" and competing are proper
goals in life.

Life is not all work. Pueblo Indians are fun-loving and sociable.
They like to get together and go visiting. There is plenty of time
for games and sports, especially during periods when little farming
is done. Some games are for men, some for women, and others for
the children. The best are those which are played by all.

Children play with toys, dolls, and beanshooters, with tops, hoops, sticks, stones, darts, and small pottery animals. They play at cat's cradle—a game taught to the people by the legendary spider woman. They play guessing games, games of chance, and games of skill.

Like everything in Pueblo life, games are part of religion. Many games are said to have been invented by the gods. This is true of the sacred foot races. In some pueblos altars are put up for the runners, who are also given special medicines. In some cases races are not run to win, but to keep the sun moving, the rivers flowing, and the corn growing.

Kick races were invented by the twin gods of war who are imagined as a pair of mischievous children. The thing kicked can be a ball, stick, stone, cylindrical piece of wood, or hairball smeared with resin. Usually two teams of four or five runners race against each other. The race covers a lot of ground, sometimes thirty or more miles. At Zuñi it is one of the greatest events. Men race all the way to Toayanala, the sacred thunder mountain, and back to the central plaza. The exicitement generated by this race is immense. The runners are solemnly blessed by a native priest. The most fleet-footed young men are chosen to compete against one another—one team from the northern part of the pueblo and one from the southern part. This is also the case in some other pueblos. At Taos, for instance, teams of summer and winter people do the racing.

Money, concho belts, silver and turquoise necklaces, bracelets and rings, horses, sheep, blankets, boots and saddles are wagered by those who root for one team or the other, with women betting as eagerly as men. Once the race starts, two or three hundred riders on horseback gallop alongside the runners—mostly bettors who cannot wait to see how their team is doing. In a kick race the stick, or ball, may not be touched by hand. This is tough on the runner, especially if the stick lands in a thorn bush or cactus clump, because the competitors are barefoot.

Practicing this game begins in childhood. Four- and five-year-olds

Foot races are held in many pueblos. They are often of a sacred nature, run to ensure rain and good crops.

play at kicking the stick as hard and far as their little feet are able. There are also relay races, usually sacred, which are run on straight courses with teams running against one another. The team that gains a lap on the other wins. Children run against other children, girl teams against girl teams, clan against clan, kiva society against kiva society, pueblo against pueblo. There are even races for married women. At Taos runners wear plumes of birds to "give them wings." In a few places the sacred races are no longer run because railroads, highways, and land development have encroached upon the ancient race courses.

Another favorite game is shinny ball, which is also played by non-Pueblo Indians. Shinny is a kind of hockey game played with curved sticks and balls made of buckskin. Some pueblos have a legend that shinny ball as well as other games were invented by the Mother goddess and that the first humans brought these games with them when they emerged from *Sipapu,* coming up from a previous world on to our earth. Shinny can be played by everybody, boys as well as girls. Even married women take a hand at it.

Shinny, like other Pueblo games, often has a religious meaning. Just as after a kick race, the kicking sticks are buried in a corn-field to make the plants grow, so shinny balls, on ceremonious occasions, are filled with seeds. It is a lucky omen if a ball bursts scattering the seeds over the ground. It means that the corn crop will be good at harvest time.

A well-loved sport is the hoop and dart, or ring game. Players roll a hoop along as fast as possible while other players try to throw their darts or sticks through the swift-moving ring. At the turn of the century George Wharton James described in his book *Indians of the Painted Desert Region* such a game played by the Hopi boys:

A game that requires considerable skill to play, is *we-la.* It consists in several players, each armed with a feathered dart, or *ma-te-va,* rushing after a small hoop woven of corn husks—the *we-la*—and throwing their darts through it. Each player's dart has a different color of feathers, so that each can tell when he scores. To see a dozen almost nude youths darting along the dance plaza, or down in the valley on the sand, laughing, shouting, gesticulating . . . eagerly following the motion of the thrower of the *we-la,* and then, suddenly letting fly the *ma-te-va,* is a picturesque and lively sight.

Many games are preparations for adult life, such as bow-and-arrow shoots and hunting games. A rabbit hunt is a sport at which women sometimes compete with men. If a woman gets a rabbit before a man she exchanges clothes with him and he has to get the next rabbit to get them back. If he cannot do this he has to gather a load of firewood for the victorious woman.

One of the roughest, most exciting games is the "chicken pull" or gallop race, which can be done either on foot or horseback. On horseback it is a mad, dangerous, and breath-taking contest. A rooster is buried in the ground so that only its head is showing, or it is suspended from a pole. Galloping at full speed, a daring rider will snatch up the bird and make off with it pursued by all the others. Then begins the mad struggle for possession of the rooster's body, a struggle in which a kneecap can be smashed or a horse's neck broken. The wild chase begins on the mesa top, hoofs clattering over slippery rocks. It goes down steep trails to the valley floors, among the cactus flats, and then up again. Riders pile into each other grabbing at a rooster wing or leg. Lummis described the race at Acoma: "Each man who captures a fragment spurs out into the valley, hounded by relentless rivals. They smite one another with full force across the face with the feathered weapon, and dark eyes flash, and blood trickles down; but big white teeth are shining in the gallant joy of the generous strife. I have never known one of these combatants to lose his temper."

Somewhere between the ages of twelve and sixteen, children undergo a rite of initiation which transforms them into adults. In the case of boys, this means becoming a member in one of the kiva societies and learning its secrets. The kivas form part of the men's world. Each pueblo has secret ceremonial societies which every boy, and in a few places, every girl, has to join.

The kiva has been called the nearest thing to the white man's high school. There, during long winter nights, the boys sit, legs drawn up and chins resting on their knees, listening to the older men, wrapped in their blankets, reciting the old tales, myths, and history, sometimes far into the night. The boys are taught the Pueblo way—by word of mouth, by listening again and again until they know the story of their people by heart.

The initiation is solemn, scary, even painful, a real test of manhood or womanhood. It represents not only a child's coming of age, but also making a bond with the gods. Before the rite, children have their hair washed with yucca. They carry the same white ear of corn given them at birth. In certain tribes, the fearful, masked whipping kachinas will come down the ladder into the kiva with whips of yucca stems and hit each child four times across the arms and legs. They strike hard, sometimes drawing blood. This is done not to punish the children, but "to take away bad happenings." It is usually the ceremonial father, often a maternal uncle, who acts as the sponsor for the youngster on this occasion. He might put himself between the whipping kachina and the child after the second blow and receive the other two himself. But if a boy has been very bad and disrespectful to his elders, his ceremonial father might not feel like doing this. After that, it is the children's turn to whip the kachinas as a symbol that they are now grown up.

Afterward, supernatural beings taking part in the initiation take off their masks and put them on those who have now become adults. Now, for the first time, boys and girls learn that the masked kachinas they have seen dancing in the plaza on ceremonial feast days are not gods, but fathers, uncles, and relatives. The youngsters are warned never to tell what they have learned in the kiva, never to reveal to smaller children that the masked dancers are not wondrous spirits. At Zuñi, they are told that one boy who gave away a kiva's secrets had his head cut off by kachinas who kicked it all the way to the sacred lake at the bottom of which they live. Secrecy about what goes on in the kiva societies is strictly maintained. There are good reasons for this. Mysteries revealed lose their power. Certain dances observed by outsiders who are not supposed to see them fail to produce rain. The suppression of Indian religion, first by the Spaniards

One of the public ceremonies, the Basket Dance at Picuris symbolizes the planting, sifting, and grinding of corn.

and later by Anglo missionaries and officials, has added to the Pueblo's custom of concealing much of their religious life from outsiders.

In some pueblos, children undergo two initiations—a preliminary one, when they are between six and nine years old, and the main one later when they are in their teens. After that they get still another adult name, and are ready to assume the responsibilities of grownups.

Among the Zuñis, a boy can take part in the masked dances. But he may not own a mask, only borrow one. He will own his personal mask and hang it up on the wall of his house only after he has married. This mask will be buried with him when he dies. In some villages boys spend long periods of time away from home within their kiva societies. "This will make them into men and not mamma's boys," as one Taos elder explained. In Hopi villages the girl who has gone through her initiation will now wear her butterfly hairdo which marks her as a young unmarried woman. The "butterfly" is almost never seen anymore, except during ceremonial dances.

Soon comes a time to think about marriage. Among whites, up to recent times, all a young woman could do was to let herself be seen and noticed by a man. It was up to the male to make the first move. It was, and usually still is, the prospective groom who does the "proposing." Not so among the Pueblos. It shows the respect for and high status of Pueblo women that the first move is often up to the girl. As Charles Lummis said, "The Pueblo invented women's rights before any white."

Among the Zuñi, courtship begins when "a girl expresses a fancy for a young man." Her parents, or some other relatives, then tell those of the boy, and they encourage him to take the next step, namely, to drop in at the house of the girl for a chat "as if by accident." First he is fed. Then the father of the girl inquires casually, "Maybe you came for something?" The boy says, "Yes, I came thinking of your daughter." To which the father usually replies, "I cannot think for her, let her speak." After that, the courtship is on.

In the Hopi pueblos, courtship was an elaborate undertaking. During a rabbit hunt, girls used to take cornmeal cakes along to trade with the boys for rabbits. At the end of a chase a girl might give all she had left to a certain boy. That meant that she liked him, liked him very much. He took them home and told his parents about it. A few days later the girl would "sit where she could be seen," grinding corn on her *metate*. If the boy then went to her house, it was considered the beginning of a romance.

After a little while the girl would take *piki*—the paper-thin, rolled up wafer bread of blue corn—to the boy's house. If he ate it, and gave some of it to his male relatives, it meant that he accepted her as his bride. He and the men in his family then began to weave beautiful white wedding robes edged in black, green, and red for the bride-to-be. She, with the help of her mother and aunts, started to grind great quantities of cornmeal for the wedding feast. With her baskets full of meal, she then went again to the boy's home grinding corn for his mother for another three days. During this time the boy's aunts staged a mock attack on his house which was the occasion of much fun and teasing. Don Talayesva described some goings-on at his marriage:

The aunts of my father's clan . . . ganged up and staged a big mud fight with the men of my family. They caught my grandfather and plastered him with mud from head to foot. They also poured mud and water all over my father . . . they made fun of Irene (the bride-to-be), calling her cross-eyed, lazy, dirty, and a poor cook, and praised me highly, asserting that they would like to have me for a husband. . . . My godmother threw mud on my father and uncles and said that she wanted me for a lover. This mud fight was to show that they were very fond of me, and that they thought Irene was making a good choice.

Before the wedding, the groom's mother washes the bride's hair with yucca suds, while the bride's mother does the same to the groom. A great feast is held. The boy's father makes a path of sacred cornmeal leading from his home to hers. The newlyweds take a pinch of cornmeal, walk silently to the eastern part of the mesa, breathe upon the cornmeal, throw it toward the rising sun, pray, and return to the village a married couple.

Modern Hopis observe much of the old wedding ritual, but usually not all of it. It would, for instance, be hard today to find many prospective young bridegrooms with the skill to weave fine wedding robes embroidered with symbols of suns and butterflies.

In most villages, a husband goes to live with his wife. Family, to the Pueblos, means a woman, or group of women, and their children and children's children—to which are added husbands and other male relatives—"a slow stream of mothers and daughters forming a current that carries with it husbands, sons, and grandsons." The role of the woman is emphasized by the fact that the house is always hers and that the children take her family name. The woman's status is further enhanced in that the image of the godhead is not necessarily a bearded father figure. "God" could be "She" like the great Corn Mother. Marriages within the same clan are forbidden. Traditionalists frown on marriages with whites or Chicanos. Still, a number of mixed marriages take place nowadays.

A woman can divorce her husband simply by putting his things outside the house, which is hers, and sending him "back to his own people." But she will do so only if she has very good reasons; otherwise, she would be shamed. Pueblo marriages are stable, and children are brought up with a great sense of security. In many villages the newlywed couple drink sacred water from a double wedding jar while a native priest prays and tells them: "Your marriage is serious and important to the whole pueblo. You must not be foolish and bicker with each other, but get along and live in harmony, so that the people whose love and respect you treasure can be proud of you. Keep this wedding olla carefully. Never drop or break it. May your marriage last as well as a good jar."

For married couples, life goes along on "Indian time," not ruled by a clock but by the natural rhythm of nature, the changing of seasons, the unending circle of birth, growth, and aging, of sowing and reaping. Men and women working among whites must live on "white man's time," but that is not natural. It is something one cannot help.

The very young and the very old—all part of the living circle of the people—the circle without beginning and without end.

Respect for old age is the cornerstone of Indian society. To grow old is not a tragedy, but something desirable which brings honor. Old people stay with the family, active and useful to the last. Getting rid of old people by putting them in an old folks' home is something a Pueblo cannot understand. Old people have so much to do— a grandfather instructs young boys in the kiva, a grandmother helps at a grandchild's birth. Let the men of other tribes dream of a warrior's death—the peaceful Pueblos hope instead for a gentle death in old age, coming unnoticed to them in their sleep.

Hell and heaven are white people's conceptions. "You invented hell," an old Indian told a missionary. "You can keep it." If a

Pueblo man or woman dies it is of course a sad occasion, but it is thought bad and foolish to have a fancy funeral and to grieve too long and too hard. Too much mourning is considered harmful because it keeps people from going about their daily tasks which keep the village alive. Besides, the dead one is going to the sun, or to *Sipapu* whence he came. He will live on in the other world as before, except that in that world, day will be night, summer will be turned into winter, and the departed will do things with their left instead of their right hands. Many people manage to believe in a Catholic heaven as well.

For the dead a road is sprinkled to guide them to the other world. They will need food and clothing there. They have their hair combed and washed and are laid out in their best garments. "We raised the body to a sitting position and combed her hair. We put on her a new dress and prayer feathers into her hand to take along to our dear departed ones, put a cloud over her face in the form of a cotton mask and wrapped her up in her beautiful wedding robe." Hopi men have their digging sticks placed into their grave, stuck in upright as a ladder from the other world.

A dead person's spirit stays around his home for four days. During this time food and drink is offered to him and mirrors are turned against the wall. Before a grave is closed, the dead will be given a last drink of the sacred water which represents survival of the people as a whole. Pottery vessels in prehistoric graves were "killed" by making a hole in them so that they could be taken along to the world of the dead. A pottery jar is still broken over each grave, and Pueblo cemeteries are always covered with pottery fragments. In some eastern pueblos such as Isleta, food is put out for the dead on All Saints Day, as relatives call out the names of those who are gone, telling them to come and eat. Bowls of corn are also placed on the graves.

Generally, however, people do not like to pronounce the name of a dead relative, and after a funeral, people will purify themselves. As a child grows up to live his or her life, so the dead must free themselves from their ties with the living, and the survivors must free themselves from them so that the spirits can depart without regret. They travel to a place prepared for them since the world began. If they have been good, holy people, they will continue to help their village by sending life-giving rain. In some places, prayers and offerings will be made to them. The living and the dead and the yet unborn continue to be part of that circle without beginning and without end which the Pueblos hope will last as long as the earth will bring forth corn and the sky clouds heavy with raindrops and as long as the sun god will give warmth and life to this world.

It has been jokingly said that Pueblo houses are built to form little plazas in which ceremonies are held and to make many flat roofs from which the dances can be watched.

# 11 ▪ UP THE LADDER, DOWN THE LADDER

*I remember my home*
*Surrounded by green cottonwoods,*
*I remember it and sing.*
*I remember how we used to live,*
*Walking, laughing, through fields of corn,*
*Climbing up and down ladders,*
*But now?*

PUEBLO POEM

A white trader once said laughingly that the Pueblos build their homes for the main purpose of grouping houses to form plazas in which ceremonies can be held. The flat roofs are made for people to sit on so that they can watch the dances. There is something to this. Pueblo houses, nestling against one another, surrounding the village square, their backs to the outside, are symbols of the people's sense of containment and inwardness.

Made of adobe, pueblo houses blend perfectly into the surrounding landscape and are ideally suited to a land of canyons and deserts, mesas and cornfields. Adobe was no novelty to the Spaniards—as a matter of fact *adobe* is a Spanish word of Arabic origin. People in southern Spain, Italy, and especially North Africa along the Mediterranean have always used house-building techniques similar to those of the Pueblos.

A pueblo used to be picturesque—a jumble of soft, rounded shapes, ladders, and beehive ovens—an artist's or photographer's paradise. Some villages such as Taos, Acoma, and the Hopi pueblos still retain much of their ancient charm.

Frank Cushing in the 1890's described the oriental look of Zuñi Pueblo, its narrow, winding passageways and irregularly shaped plazas, houses piled one upon the other to a height of four, five, or

Ladders, ladders everywhere. In the old villages people spent a considerable time climbing up and down ladders to enter or leave their houses
through the rooftop. Here is a Hopi woman in 1908.

even six stories, forming a gigantic adobe honeycomb, the contrast of
light and shadow, red chilis drying on strings, the terraces and rooftops populated by gossiping, laughing women shucking corn, smoke
rising from innumerable chimneys made of bottomless earthen pots
set on top of one another and cemented together with mud, the small

Old and new in one picture. A traditional, centuries-old building in Acoma. A scene from yesterday, except for the girl's modern dress. The picture was taken in 1955.

windows looking wonderfully like tiny holes in an anthill. He commented on the delicious smell of newly baked bread emanating from numberless round-topped adobe ovens. He noted the many ladders leading from one terraced rooftop to the one above. He spoke of ladders leaning against the buildings everywhere, each stretching

The typical old pueblo, in this case a Zuñi village in 1879. A jumble of terraces and ladders with many chimneys made of clay pots piled up on one another.

two thin arms skyward. He was especially impressed with the acrobatic nimbleness of the Zuñi people:

> All the inhabitants have a sailor-like agility in the use of the ladders. The women go up and down with water jars on their heads without touching a hand to support and steady themselves; little children, hardly out of babyhood, scramble fearlessly up and down; even the dogs have a squirrel-like nimbleness, trotting in a matter-of-course way down the rungs of a steep ladder.

The Pueblos did not have to buy material for their homes; it lay under their feet. In the pueblos along the Rio Grande, houses were made entirely of adobe. In pueblos built on or near rocky mesas, such as Acoma, Zuñi, and the Hopi towns, the core of a building was often made of masonry—chipped or split stones laid in rows, the cracks filled in with mud and the whole plastered over with adobe. Abode is a clayish earth mixed with sand and straw to give it firmness. It dries hard, without cracking. It is a fine building material and costs nothing.

"Our houses," says Santana Antonio from Acoma, "are almost living, breathing things. They change forever, as human beings change from childhood to old age. In the old days you couldn't enter a house from the ground floor. You had to climb up one ladder, and then another, to the roof of the highest floor, the third floor. Then you climbed ladders again, down, inside. This was a protection against wild raiders, Navajos and Apaches. If enemies came, we simply drew the ladders up—and then what could they do? In some places I know of, Zuñi for instance, a house expands when a daughter marries and and extra room is needed. Then the house grows sideways or upward.

"Our homes are warm in winter and cool in the summer. They are waterproof, but a tiny mouse could cause damage. Houses change all the time. Sometimes the outside starts to crumble here and there exposing the stone or wood, but so what? We just smear a little adobe over here, do some plastering over there. Even the old church looks different now from the photos taken of it eighty years ago. Since then the adobe and stone bricks have been covered and the whole structure looks nice, smooth and thicker than it did before. We build our houses like we make pottery, with our bare hands and layers upon layers of wet earth. Really, our houses are big pieces of pottery." Houses were built so that the second story receded, making the front half of the first-floor roof a balcony. At Acoma the three main streets of ancient houses have been likened to "three rows of giant steps."

At Acoma and elsewhere one can still find in some buildings small windowpanes made of mica or isinglass—a kind of natural mineral that comes in layers. This mica is not as transparent as modern glass, but it does let some daylight through. Mica windowpanes were used before the coming of white people, and for a long time after. These days, of course, Pueblo Indians buy their windows, glass and all, from stores and place them in their adobe structures.

Over three hundred years ago the Spanish friar Benavides wrote: "For among these nations it is the custom for the women to build the walls; and the men spin. . . . And if we try to oblige some man to build a wall, he runs away from it; and the women laugh."

The Hopi Don Talayesva said: "Almost everyone in the village helped me on the house. My dear, old mother helped bring loads of dirt, and my blind old father did all that he could and wove a Hopi blanket for me. We all had a fine feast in the new house."

Today both men and women usually work on the building of a house—the men cutting and bringing the heavy timber, especially the roof beams, the *vigas*—but the main work is still done by women. George Wharton James described the building of a Hopi house around the turn of the century:

Without plumb-line, straight line, or trowel they proceed. Some women bringing earth, sand, or limestone rocks . . . in baskets, buckets, or dish pans. Others mix the adobe to the proper consistency and see that the workers are kept supplied with it. And, what a laughing chattering group it is. Every tongue seems to be going and no one listening.

Then came the finishing of the house:

With a small heap of adobe mud the woman, using her hand as a trowel, fills in the chinks, smooths and plasters the walls inside and out. Splashed from head to foot with mud, she is an object to behold, and, if her children are there to "help" her, no mudlarks ever looked more happy . . . then, when the whitewashing is done with gypsum, or the coloring of the walls, what fun the children have—as they splash their tiny hands into the coloring matter and dash it upon the walls.

House building is largely women's work, at Taos and elsewhere.

Here is a man from Jemez digging clay to make adobe bricks.

Adobe walls, forever crumbling and forever renewed, have a character of their own.

Pueblos do not have to be told about recycling materials. They have practiced this for hundreds of years. Materials from an old, abandoned house are often used to build a new one. Interior walls are sometimes whitewashed with a rabbit-fur mitten dipped in paint. Walls used to be decorated with animal and other designs. In some pueblos a small patch of the wall is left unplastered. The Kachinas will come and cover it with invisible plaster.

If a traditional Hopi wants to build a house, this intention is announced by the town crier. Friends, especially clan brothers and sisters, bring materials and willing hands to help. Four eagle feathers are offered up in prayer and placed beneath the cornerstones of the house. Sacred cornmeal and food crumbs are sprinkled between these stones outlining the floor of the house to be built. The Hopi house song is sung. Later, prayer sticks are placed among the roof beams. When the roof is finished, crumbs of food are also strewn along the beams "to feed the house" and keep its inhabitants from want.

Among the Zuñis a big new house is built each year to receive the blessings of the masked gods who enter the house during the Shalako winter festival. The owner has to ask all his relatives to help him put up a house for the Shalako and feed them while they are at work. Such a house, entered by the gods, will be a lucky one. Many Zuñi homes came into being this way.

Naturally, more modern homes are built nowadays than traditional ones. The U.S. government has sponsored a number of low-cost housing projects. At Tesuque, for instance, a contractor for the government put up twenty-five dwellings, most of the labor performed by the Indians who would inhabit them. Each house had a modern kitchen, bathroom, central heating, and electricity. In many villages people have a choice: Give up some of the old ways in order

Nobody is too small to help make adobe bricks in Jemez.

to have Anglo comforts, or be traditional and do without many things white Americans take for granted. It is a choice each man or woman will have to make at some time in their lives.

The interior of a home is always very neat, uncluttered, and spotlessly clean. One of the most important things in every house is the adobe fireplace in the corner. Another essential household item is the *metate* and *mano* for grinding corn, though few families now depend upon a grinding stone for their daily meal.

Furniture is extremely simple; nothing is superfluous. In the old days the Pueblos did entirely without beds, tables, and chairs. Along one wall ran an adobe bench to be used as a shelf or a place to sit. Otherwise, much of the living was done on the floor. A layer of blankets was the bed. Rolled up, it became a chair. A long pole hanging down from the ceiling served as a clothes rack. Antlers driven into the wall served as clothes pegs. What the Pueblo woman needed in the way of cooking utensils she made herself. She had many pottery jars, most important the big, beautifully painted ollas in which the drinking water was kept. Porous and moist on the outside, the ollas kept water wonderfully cool even in the hot summer.

Water generally was fetched from a well, a stream, or a waterhole. The huge waterhole at Acoma, formed of gigantic rocks and cliffs, was a natural cistern catching enough rainwater and snow in fall and winter to last the pueblo through the dry season. It was a grand sight to see the women of Acoma climbing up and down the ancient steps and faint footholds chipped into the rock, gracefully balancing large ollas on their heads without spilling a drop.

At Zuñi an early visitor thought that the scene around the village pool was right out of the Bible: "Here in the cool shadow crowds of girls come and go, dipping up the water, and pausing to gossip as they meet in the path or beside the well. Their soft voices fill the air like the chatter of swallows, and their white teeth gleam as they laugh."

A modern Pueblo. Jemez, New Mexico.

These scenes are seen now only in one's memory. Today many Pueblo homes have tap water. In their rooms they have chairs, tables, and beds. The linoleum on the floor is covered by a colorful Mexican rug. They have washing machines. Before the coming of electricity, these were often coal-powered. On the walls are mirrors, and family photos, as well as pictures of saints or bright-tinted missionary cards. Sometimes a cross hangs next to a kachina doll. The oven is no longer a hot stone, but either a wood-fired kitchen range or a modern gas stove. The old, beehive-shaped mud ovens, however, still turn out delicious, nicely browned bread. As an old Pueblo proverb says, "Fill your stomach and your face will brighten."

(1) Fresh bread for the whole family—homemade, natural, good to eat.

(2) Beehive-shaped ovens are still widely used to bake bread. A fire is made then fire and ashes are swept out and, while the oven is still hot . . .

(3) . . . a long-handled wooden tray is used to take the bread in and out of the oven.

(4) If visitors come at the right time, they can buy delicious, freshly baked bread from this young Taos lady.

The food, too, is now often store-bought white people's food. Still, some mouth-watering Pueblo dishes continue to be favorites—fry bread, tortillas, wild-sage bread, Pueblo enchiladas, piñon nut cakes, Acoma corn pudding, fried green chili pepper stew, frijoles with cheese and onions, baked pumpkin, spring lamb stew–Zuñi style, corn dumplings, juniper beef stew, atole cornmeal gruel, squash-blossom mush, hot pork with garlic, and many others. In the 1880s a white visitor might have been served a dish of roasted locusts, as delicate and delicious as shrimps, with a similar flavor. If that makes you shudder, you might reflect about the horror with which a Pueblo Indian will watch a white person eating snails, oysters, lobsters, frogs' legs, or, for that matter, limburger cheese. What is considered good eating is generally what one is accustomed to.

One recipe deserves to be written out—the making of wafer called *piki*—because it is the most characteristic of all Pueblo foods. It is made nowhere else in the world. *Piki* is made from blue corn—and it is *really blue.* Here is what it takes to make good *piki:*

> Blue cornmeal
> a ladle-full of sage ashes to give the
> piki its traditional color.
> Mutton tallow
> water

Boil a quart of water. Add an equal amount of finely ground blue cornmeal. Stir mixture until it thickens. Make a paste of a cupful of sage ashes and one of hot water. Sift this into roughly two quarts of blue cornmeal. Stir. Make the whole mixture into a dough and knead well until it is stiff. Add water to the dough until it has the consistency of thin batter, like dipping your hand into applesauce.

You now have everything to make *piki,* but this does not mean that you will be able to make it. That takes a special skill.

*Piki* is baked on a smooth slab of sandstone, its surface soaked, maybe for generations, in the oil of sunflower and squash seeds and

Two basic tasks performed by Hopi women in 1893: grinding corn flour and baking *piki,* the famous wafer bread.

animal fat. After each use it is rubbed down with aromatic juniper and pine boughs. The fire underneath the stone must be just right. If it is not hot enough, the food will not be done. If it is too hot, the stone will crack and that would shame the cook and be taken as a bad sign.

As one Hopi woman says, "The slab must be just as hot as an old-fashioned laundry iron used to starch a shirt. It must hiss and sizzle when you spread the *piki* mixture over it." When both stone and batter are ready the woman lightly rubs the stone with tallow, then dips her fingers into the bowl of batter and swiftly and skillfully

Making the blue-corn *piki* at the Hopi village of Hotevila today. Preparing the batter.

sweeps it over the slab with the palms of her right hand, spreading it very thinly, covering the whole stone. Almost instantly the *piki* is cooked. With her thumbs and forefingers the woman lifts it up like a piece of paper and at once repeats the whole process. When she has made enough *piki,* she rolls up the individual pieces, putting them on a flat, handsomely woven basket, ready to be served to her guests. It looks so easy that many a white visitor will say, "I can do that. Let me try." And the hostess politely will make room for the guest to try her hand. The result is always a sharp cry of pain and a few well-blistered fingers. Spreading the batter with your bare hand seems something only a Pueblo woman can do.

Clothing and appearance rank second in importance, next to food,

Lifting the paper-thin *piki* deftly from the hot stone without burning one's fingers takes a lot of practice.

to men and women alike. The Pueblos were almost alone among North American Indian tribes to spin, weave, and dye cotton. Woven fiber sandals were in use at the dawn of history. Before the Spaniards came, Pueblo dress was very simple. A loincloth and sandals for men, maybe a "shirt"—a piece of cotton with a hole in the middle to stick one's head through—in cold weather a feather blanket or some animal fur as a wraparound. Women dressed almost as simply.

After the introduction of sheep by the Spaniards, wool became the favorite material. The traditional Pueblo costume evolved during the Spanish rule. Men kept wearing a loincloth, or sometimes a buckskin kilt, never adopting trousers or sleeves; but embroidered cotton or wool shirts came into fashion, gathered around the waist with a colorful sash. There was no need for much sewing, or for buttons or zippers. Shirts and wraparound bankets were mostly white, black, or dark blue. Red tradecloth of soft wool, made in England and introduced by the Spaniards, was eagerly sought because the Indians had no natural bright-red dye. The tradecloth was unraveled into yarn to be rewoven into belts or ornamental borders. At some time or other Pueblo men began wearing buckskin leggings, or knee-high moccasins possibly adopted from the Navajos. Men wore their hair in bangs, shouder-length at the side and back. Many still do. Hair in the back is sometimes gathered up in a knot tied with red or white wool strings. Headbands are popular. The typical high-crowned, wide-brimmed, black "uncle Joe" hat is still worn by many. At Taos, men often wear a sort of turban and wrap themselves in large blankets which cover their heads. Many visitors say that Taos reminds them of an Arab village out of *1001 Nights.*

From about 1880 on, Pueblo men began wearing trousers, though traditional Taos men remove the seat, wearing a combination of pants and breechcloth. Levi's, cowboy shirts, and boots are also very popular. Pants legs are sometimes slit so that men can wear high moccasins or boots under them.

The women's main garment was the manta, a simple knee-length tunic of black wool—leaving the left shoulder bare. For generations the manta was all a Pueblo woman wore. During the last century, Pueblo women took to wearing imported, wide-sleeved, pink and turquoise silk blouses underneath their mantas on festive occasions. Later they took to wearing colorfully patterned and fringed Spanish-type shawls, or mantillas, to cover their heads and shoulders. A typical part of a woman's apparel were her botas—moccasins and leg wraps made from a single piece of gleamingly whitened buck-skin wound spirally around the leg from ankle to knee. At a fiesta women also like to display their fine silver and turquoise jewelry—

Young Hopi women in the 1890s. They wear black tunics called mantas, leaving the left shoulder bare. They have sashes around their waists and fringed shawls covering their shoulders. Two of them also wear botas—moccasins and wraparound leggings made of a single piece of deer hide. They have their hair done up in the "butterfly" style worn by unmarried girls.

a profusion of squash-blossom necklaces, concho belts, huge bracelets, rings, and earrings. At today's prices this jewelry, handed down from mother to daughter, may represent a value of thousands of dollars.

Modern Pueblo women and girls wear Anglo dress nowadays. As early as 1900 Charles Lummis lamented: "Now and then one sees

Taos men also walk around wrapped in light blankets, giving their pueblo an Oriental flavor.

an Acoma woman pitifully changed from the beautiful, national costume to an American dress—even to the shoes and stockings— and it is a sight for artists to weep over."

Let us not weep too soon. On any feast day or ceremonial the old

Modern fiesta day at Acoma: a pink satin blouse, black manta, red sash, purple shawl, and lots of silver and turquoise jewelry.

costumes and jewelry come out of their hiding places and the sight of men and women dancing in their ancient finery is still a breath-taking one—snowy boots, bright silk sleeves, snowy botas, turquoise and coral and silver glisten in the sun.

Pueblo farmers can grow corn in forbidding dry lands such as this—
even in sand dunes. But it takes the right kind of corn, the right kind
of irrigation, and the right kind of care.

# 12 ▪ GREEN CORNSTALKS AND
##   GREEN DOLLAR BILLS

*Corn is the Hopi's heart*

OLD PROVERB

People must work in order to live. In the old days, for the Pueblo Indian to feed his family was a never-ending circle of planting and reaping, a task in which both men and women played an equally vital role. Life was simple, but this did not mean that it was easy.

Water was the key to survival, and the Pueblo Indian learned to hoard water as a miser hoards gold. Don Talayesva wrote of his childhood:

I also learned that water is as precious as food. Everybody appeared happy after a rain. We small boys rolled around naked in the mud puddles, doused each other with water, and built little irrigated gardens. In this way we used too much of the water from the little pond on the west side of the village where the women went to wash their clothes and the men to water their stock. Our parents scolded us for wasting water.

Men and women taking part in a ceremony were told to "think of rain while you dance." Prayers were sung on these occasions:

> *Ho wondrous water*
> *Ho wondrous water*
> *Giving new life to the drinker*
> *Giving new life to the drinker*
> *Behold southeast clouds bringing rain!*
> *Behold southeast clouds bringing rain!*
> *Bringing life to the one who drinks.*
> *Ho, wondrous water*
> *Ho, wondrous water*
> *Giving life to the people.*

227

Rain is all-important. Without it, life as the Pueblos know it will come to a stop. Ceremonial dances are, in effect, prayers for rain. This is a rain dance performed at Zuñi in 1899.

Only those Pueblos situated along the Rio Grande could be reasonably sure of getting enough water for their fields. Villages along the river's branches had to rely on rainfall for at least half the moisture their fields needed. In times of drought all could be in trouble. Every drop was precious to the desert pueblos, such as the Hopi villages, situated in a land of no visible water supply, where they could discover neither lake nor stream. Necessity and a stubborn love of their country made the Pueblos into some of the world's finest dry farmers. Some learned to plant corn among sand dunes because these retained water and formed windbreakers against storms. They utilized the spring runoffs as well as flash floods, channeling them into irrigation ditches that were deep and narrow to prevent evaporation. They invented "waffle gardens," so named by whites because, from afar, they looked like griddle cakes—tiny adjacent plots that were lovingly watered by hand for a small but dependable harvest. They labored unceasingly to maintain their irrigation systems and to carry water down from the mountains to their thirsty fields. All these methods had already been used by the Anasazi.

Water always is foremost in the Pueblos' minds. That is why depletion of lakes and streams close to their sources, even if far from Pueblo fields, is such a terrible threat to Indian survival. In the Southwest this is also why the massive, wasteful use of Hopi and Navajo water by strip miners is both a tragedy and a political issue.

Until fairly recent times, everything revolved around corn. It used to furnish 80 percent of the food the Indians ate. Upon becoming an adult a young Pueblo might be told: "Corn is our mother, the giver of life to our people—and it is the Cloud People who are the only ones to nourish it and to make it grow. They come from the four directions of the universe, they come from above and below to look into our hearts to see if we are worthy. You are grown now, and you must stay at home and work hard in your fields, as we, your elders have done, as your sons will do in time. The whites have taught us many useful things, given us many useful tools, but do not rely on them alone. Rely on the old ways of working with the earth, because these ways are eternal."

Planting is a sacred undertaking. Hopi women throw water on

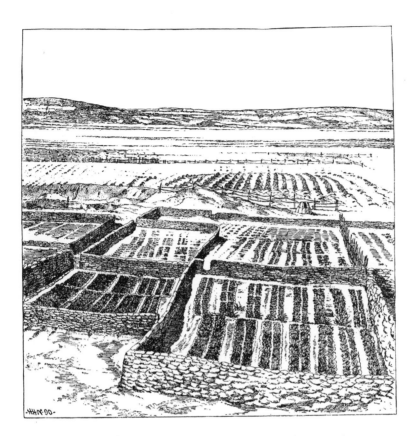

The so-called "waffle gardens" in an engraving done by an early visitor at Zuñi.

the men as they go out to plant. This will make sure that rain will fall. Often a special, ceremonial fawnskin bag is used for the seed corn which is mixed with sacred things, paint, and flower pollen. Zuñis put feather sticks in the fields as prayers for the corn. In a few eastern pueblos twigs of evergreen are used for the same purpose. Even during the winter Zuñi people will take six perfect ears of corn, hold them up in a basket, and sing to them. This is known as "dancing the corn." It is believed that the corn likes this, that it wants to be remembered even in the season when nothing grows.

Prayers are said to the corn: "Mother, Father, you among the great beings, you out of the storm clouds, help me! Help me putting down the yellow corn, and likewise the blue corn, the red and the white corn. Today, now, I am going to plant. Ease my labor. Make it not too heavy to bear. Soften the earth."

The Pueblos did not just plant plain and simple corn. They had many different varieties; the Hopis had no less than sixteen. Pueblo farmers bred special strains for different needs: desert corn that thrived with a minimum of water; corn that could be kept for years in a storage bin; corn that was delicious, but had to be eaten at once; corn that could be made into extremely fine meal; and corn for cattle. Some families were proud of the kinds that only they had developed. When one of their men married into another family, he might bring a few precious kernels with him to be planted in his wife's field as a wedding gift to herself and her clan.

The Indian farmer's tools were simple. Most of the work was done with the greasewood digging stick, unchanged since prehistoric times and in use long after the coming of the whites. Many are still used today by traditional men who say that the earth does not like the feel of iron and is harmed by it. Until the Spaniards arrived, the Pueblos had no beasts of burden. In the course of time, Indians acquired the burro to carry and the oxen to plow. The plow was usually a trimmed and cut-down tree fork. Huge and primitive, it nevertheless did its job.

The Spaniards also introduced the *carreta*—a big, lumbering, creaking cart with two oversized wheels which looked like round tabletops. Early travelers commented on the picturesque scenes in and around a pueblo, with the street full of braying burros, little children perched high on an overloaded *carreta,* three or four laughing boys riding a single pony. The burros are still there, but the ox-drawn *carreta* has long since disappeared. Most farming families now have a pickup truck, and nine times out of ten its color is turquoise—the favorite color. Today's Indian farmers also use modern tools and farm machinery, but on a modest scale.

Men and boys tended, and still tend, the cornfields; women and girls, the kitchen garden. Men made holes up to eighteen inches deep with their digging sticks so that the corn roots could get down to the moisture. Every handful of earth was carefully tended, each plant in its own place surrounded by a ridge to hold water. In the old days fields radiated out from six sacred ceremoniously planted kernels of different corn.

Corn was the main crop, but not the only one. Even before the Spaniards came the Pueblos planted squash, pumpkins, and some varieties of beans. The Spaniards introduced fruit and some European vegetables. The Anglos brought still more. Now the Pueblos grow onions, watermelons, tomatoes, wheat, beets, lettuce, cabbage, cucumbers, radishes, turnips, and carrots. There are apple, pear, apricot, and especially peach orchards in many villages. Some Hopis grow almonds.

In spite of this wealth of fruits and vegetables, the Pueblos do not neglect wild plants. As their ancestors did a thousand years ago, they pick cactus fruits, wild potatoes, cattail, yucca, and berries. Women organize parties to go up into the hills to collect piñon nuts. Men travel far to fetch salt from sacred places. Men also still go on annual hunts, though wild game now makes up only a small part of the Indians' diet. Hunting is an old tradition not easily given up. Men still pray and purify themselves for their quest of game and wear hunting charms which ensure success. After an animal is slain, the hunter must cleanse himself again, because the shedding of blood, even of a rabbit, is a serious matter. A killed deer is often covered with a blanket. Beads are placed around its neck, prayer feathers strung from antler to antler. It is asked to forgive its killer. It is thanked that it gave its flesh so that the people might live. White men also introduced domestic animals and livestock raising, but this

For over a thousand years Pueblo farmers have adapted themselves to a land of little water, wresting a livelihood from the arid soil.

happened so long ago that it has now become part of the old Indian tradition. The Pueblos raise sheep, goats, horses, and cattle, though theirs is not ideal cattle country.

The traditional way of making a living—farming, hunting, raising stock—was hard work. A Pueblo elder once told me what he had to do to feed his family:

It was always chopping weeds, pruning fruit trees, planting, digging, plowing, keeping away birds and crows from the plants, threshing wheat with horses, bringing roof beams to build houses, learning to drive a car, learning about soil conservation, learning to run a tractor. First we were what the white man calls "subsistence farmers"—that is, we raised enough to feed ourselves, maybe have a little over to do some trading. Then the white man showed us so many things he convinced us that we couldn't live without that we had to raise cash crops and become "scientific" farmers to get the money to pay for them. There wasn't enough land for that, or for our rising population either, and so, now we are back to subsistence farming and may have a white man's job also—like doing some fire-fighting on the side, or some jewelry work for the tourists. In most villages around here we Indians can no longer make a living just by farming.

Then there was the livestock. It meant for me getting out in cold, in snow, in rain, in sleet, during hailstorms, taking care of the sheep. You got to watch them all the time. They eat something wrong and get bloated. If they are that way they fall on their back, sticking up their four feet in the air, swelling up like a balloon. If that happens they can't get up by themselves and just die in a very short time. You have to "stick" them with the tip of the knife and then the air goes out "pffft," you turn the sheep over and it goes on munching grass as if nothing happened. There is the shearing in April, and getting the wool to the trader, the wrangling over money—I used to let my wife do that, she was better at it than me—and the once-a-year fight with the government man who wants to reduce your stock because of "overgrazing." We have too many sheep for the little land remaining, or rather too little grass. But if we cut down the herd we might not have enough sheep to make a living on. I also had to butcher and skin. I did not particularly like doing it, but people have to eat. You white people never see the killing, just the lamb chop.

Lambing time is a busy time. You have to keep off dogs and coyotes, hand-carry the lambs until they can keep up with the flocks. Mark mother and baby with paint to match them up when they don't recognize each other, which happens. Squirt milk on a lamb to make the mother lick it and acknowledge it as her own. At lambing time my mother used to come out and cook and feed us, setting up a sheep camp with her tent. I never learned to spin or weave, though, like my father did. I don't think there is anyone left I know in our pueblo who can do it.

But, I knew how to raise horses, how to race them and build corrals for them. I kept chickens and grew peaches. At the end of April, I planted melons, squash, and beans. In May mushmelon, watermelons, and lima beans. By the end of June I had put in the main crop of corn. I worked in many ways to guard my plants from pests. We had natural things to spray our plants with to keep them away, but seldom altogether. I fought the bugs. I saw my plants being nibbled away by rabbits, my seeds eaten by birds. I had to be ever watchful. I ran races to encourage the corn to grow rapidly. I shot deer on Mount Taylor.

I worked for white ranchers for cash and, for a while at the railroad yards in Winslow. I castrated my rams and stallions with the help of brothers and uncles. I liked this even less than butchering, but this is part of livestock work. Finally, I learned how to repair the pickup truck, which really belongs to my son. The sweet corn was harvested first, beans last. Before the harvest was brought in our village was swept, cleaned, and purified. Then we danced. Oh, yes, I learned my dancing, and all the old songs, did my duties in the kiva, filled the offices to which I was appointed, and will fill others still. Yes, my friend, I have had a very busy life, but I think my wife was even busier than me. I won't even try to think of all the different things she had to do.

The traditional way of life no longer can provide for all the Pueblos. In the economy of the villages farming plays an ever smaller role, though the religious ceremonies still revolve around it. The Pueblos must look for other means to make a livelihood. Many men and women have turned to crafts. Zuñi Pueblo derives its main income now from producing some of the finest Indian jewelry. The jewelers of Santo Domingo are not only known for their silver, coral, and turquoise necklaces—called *hishi*—but also for their skill in marketing them. Many Pueblo women make a nice income from pottery. Increasingly Pueblo Indians have to leave their villages in order to find work, as unemployment at home is as high as 40 percent. Tribal

Many Pueblo men and women now make their living outside their villages in modern, sophisticated jobs. This young X-ray technician works in the Indian hospital at Albuquerque, New Mexico.

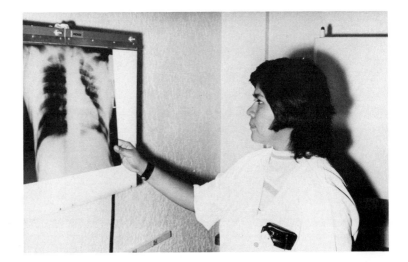

governments and the Federal Bureau of Indian Affairs employ a few people. The Bureau operates under an "Indian preference" rule under which Native Americans should have first chance at a job. But often a white is hired rather than an Indian with the excuse that the white applicant "has had better training and education." If that is the case, whose fault is it? Certainly not the Indians'. If they get jobs at all, they are often the lowest paid.

In 1971 the Arizona Highway Department had 42 Indians working for it—42 out 4277 employees! In the Anglo world the Pueblos have to compete with others in the job market. They have to cope with discrimination. They have to fight to be accepted by certain unions who would like to keep Indians out. Many jobs are open only to union members. They have to adjust to a world ruled by the clock and the wristwatch. The Pueblo has made progress. A man from San Juan is a licensed building contractor; his firm employs mostly Indians. A man from San Juan is a renowned anthropologist, teacher, and lecturer. A man from Jemez is a health officer as well as government official, artist, and writer. Pueblo men and women have become successful technicians, teachers, ranchers, and businessmen.

They work as keypunch operators, or in a Winslow, Arizona, garment factory. They run tractors. Zuñis have won citations for outstanding work in fire-fighting which has cost the lives of some brave men. Pueblos own and work in stores and gas stations. They work in motels. They work in Los Alamos—"Atom City"—where Pueblo Indians from many villages meet.

There are tribal enterprises. The Hopis have estabished an industrial park, Cochiti, a farm and ranching cooperative, and also a development committee. Isleta has a packing company on the reservation. Laguna is rich in mineral resources. Anaconda's jackpile open-pit uranium mine is situated on Laguna land, and the Pueblo receives a yearly income from it. These enterprises have sprung up not because the Pueblos are fond of them, but because today they

In some pueblos the land alone can no longer support the people. Zuñi men, as well as those of other pueblos, earn money fighting the nation's forest fires. Crews sign up before boarding a plane, to put out brush fires in California.

live in a world in which even the most traditional Pueblo elder must have some money to buy a shirt, a raincoat, sugar, coffee, a window-pane, or to pay for a bus trip, a postage stamp, a box of matches, a sickle, a knife, or a hunting rifle.

For most of their history the Pueblos lived without this strange thing called money—even after the Spaniards came and for some time after the Anglos arrived. Indians have learned what a dollar is for. Still, it is hard for them, especially for the traditional Pueblo, to adjust to white concepts of time and money. People ate when their bodies told them it was time to eat, not in obedience to the hands on a clock. They did their planting when the sun watcher told them it was time to plant, not when a calendar or a scientific book said so. The idea that land could be worked for an individual's profit, that a man could take out a deed for it, that it could be used for anything except for the benefit of all according to the will of the Ones Above was, and to a certain extent still is, alien to them. In fact, any idea of personal ownership beyond clothing, ornaments, weapons, or sacred things was till recently strange to men who never had any property, who were used to the fact that even the deer they killed and brought home belonged to their wives the moment it was carried into the house. Neither can the Pueblo's love of simplicity tolerate the cluttering up of a home with gadgets. He cannot understand a politician running for office, and it goes against his grain to practice a sport merely to best an opponent. His work philosophy, as well as his philosophy about other things in life, is generally in conflict with Anglo attitudes about the same subject, whether it is a job, money, religious belief, man-woman relationships, child rearing, old age, or the meaning of life.

"Bahana, our white brother," said an old Hopi man, "was supposed to bring us the missing piece of our sacred tablet. Instead he brought us the dollar bill. It can't be fitted to the tablet." Yet Pueblos work at Los Alamos and go home to sing in their kivas. When in 1901 the people of Acoma agreed to a sheep reduction ordered by the government, Charles Lummis saw in this the imminent breakup of their pueblo. "Acoma," he wrote, "will soon be only a ruin for tourists."

Old Acoma is not inhabited any more. It is too much trouble for the people to live up on the old rock and then come down and travel many miles to fields or sheep camps. Old Acoma is no place to commute from. But when the time for certain ceremonies comes, the houses magically fill with people, the drums beat in the kivas, the voice of the town crier resounds in streets empty of tourists. Those who have pronounced the death of the pueblos and the disappearance of the tribes almost yearly for the past two centuries have failed to take into account the resilience of the Pueblo Indians who are not so much protected by walls of brick, which can be smashed, but by walls of desert sand which give way but render a blow ineffective.

"Look at the highway," says an old Acoma woman. "You people have paved over our world. But under the concrete, seeds are sprouting. Look, the strength of that herb over there, that flower here, is greater than that of the layers of concrete. The highway cracks and the flower comes through. You can pave it over and over again. It does not matter. What seems so strong and powerful is acutally weak. That which seems weak and hardly noticeable has strength. The concrete pavement is dead. The flower is alive. Life in the end wins out. This world might be destroyed. It will not be destroyed by us. If it should happen, we shall find another *Sipapu,* a way to another world. But enough of that. Let's have some coffee."

# 13 ▪ CLAY AND TURQUOISE

*Art comes from the heart.*
*Our old arts and crafts will*
*continue to be made as long as*
*there are Indians left on this earth.*

SANTANA ANTONIO

Indian art is flourishing as never before. At auctions southwestern Indian arts and crafts, especially traditional jewelry, bring fantastic prices. The times when Indian jewelers or potters worked for 15 cents an hour are over. Whites have discovered the value of Native American art, but so have the Indians. Among the best craftsmen and artists are the Pueblos. Their art is timeless, having its roots in the world of the Anasazi.

Basketry is the oldest of all Pueblo arts; not without reason were the people of one of the earliest cultures in the Southwest called Basket Makers. Except for a few simple, utilitarian plaited yucca baskets produced in Jemez, the only Pueblo baskets made nowadays are the work of Hopi women. Baskets play a role in the traditional life of the people. They are used in the women's basket dance. Before a wedding, a Hopi bride and her mother make many baskets. The bride, followed by relatives carrying baskets full of cornmeal, walks to the house of her groom-to-be. These wedding baskets are given to his mother, all except the biggest, carried by the bride herself, which is given to the groom to keep until his death when it will be buried with him.

The Hopis live on three mesas, outcroppings of a high plateau, which jut out into the desert like three giant fingers. Hopi basketry is different in color and design from mesa to mesa. One produces wickerwork trays, bowls, wastebaskets of rabbit brush or sumac colored with native dyes and aniline. Another mesa is known for tightly woven, coiled trays and baskets of grass sewn with narrow strips of natural vegetable-dyed yucca. Some villages make twined "peach baskets," gathering baskets, and finely woven watertight baskets. Even within the same village, baskets reflect the individuality of the maker. No piece is ever exactly like another. All Hopi villages make plaited sifting baskets constructed on a willow ring sometimes reinforced with thin wire. This type of basket was being made fifteen hundred years ago. Some baskets have a characteristic "hump" in the center which is typically Hopi. Baskets are not primarily made for tourists, but to be used in Hopi households. Only the surplus is sold. Pueblo crafts are living art forms, not museum pieces.

Hopi women use many different designs on their baskets: whirlwind, lightning, and sun symbols; eagles; antelopes; snakes; kachina masks; dancing gods; and geometric patterns. For coloring, clay or rock is ground on a flat stone into paint and mixed with the oil of well-chewed squash seeds. Iron ochers and green, copper-containing rocks are used for this. Vegetable colors are made from alder bark, sumac berries, and saffron flowers. Black is achieved by mixing boiled sunflower seeds with piñon gum. The paint is often applied with a rabbit's foot.

Twining is done by weaving two strands in and out, over and under, through a system of foundation strands that are twisted together whenever they connect. Hopi brides take their blankets home in a rolled-up twined reed mat or door curtain.

Coiling is another ancient Basket Maker technique now used only by the Hopis. The foundation of a coiled basket is an ever-growing spiral of tough, stiff grass or bendable flexible plant stem. Around this, softer, narrower grasses of different colors are wound.

Plaiting is done with more pliant reeds and grasses. Cattails and split yucca leaves are used for this process; the leaves are kept moist and soft by burying them in wet sand. In plaiting, the fingers weave

Vera Pouyouma of Hotevila surrounded by her traditional Hopi baskets.
She uses methods inherited from her grandmother for her basketry.

stiff twigs in a wickerwork pattern. Carrying baskets are made in this
way. Hopi baskets are a tasteful combination of form, color, and design—a delight to the eye.

Weaving is an art closely allied to basketry. Again, only in the
Hopi villages is it still being done to any extent. As a traditional

craft, weaving has died out among the other Pueblos. People must now go to the Hopis for the ceremonial sashes used on feast days.

Cotton weaving was practiced by the Anasazis as early as A.D. 800. Around 1600 they began to use wool, and in the nineteenth century commercial yarn. Much of the yarn is still handspun on a spindle. Only rarely does one find a loom in a Hopi house. Men seem to do their weaving mostly in kivas now, especially of belts or garments intended for use during sacred dances.

A loom is a system of foundation strands—called the warp—strung between two beams. The beam nearest the weaver is called the cloth beam, while the one at the farther end is known as the yard beam. The Hopis use two kinds of looms: the big, upright blanket loom and the smaller waist loom for making belts and sashes. The yard beam of a waist loom can be attached to a tree, a peg in the wall, or a post; the cloth beam is attached to the weaver's body around the hips. Thus the weaver becomes in fact part of the loom. Hopi men wear striped woollen blankets; boys, plaid blankets; maidens, red- and blue-bordered shawls, braided sashes, and embroidered wedding robes.

The third of the ancient Pueblo arts is pottery making and it is thriving. Good Pueblo wares are much-sought collector's items. The women potters find it a good source of income. Ceramics are made in many villages; they each have their own, distinct style.

San Ildefonso is famous for its highly polished blackware, made popular by Maria Martiñez, the renowned "potter from San Idlefonso." Variations are black-on-black pottery in which the background is shiny and the designs a dull matte. In another type the designs are carved into the surface. Some pottery combines both processes.

Santa Clara has blackware almost identical to that of San Ildefonso. Their matte-on-luster pottery is probably inspired by San Ildefonso techniques. Santa Clarans sometimes impress into their vessels

Most weaving is traditionally done by men. In rare cases, Zuñi women
wove belts on a waist loom. Weaving is a dying art among the Pueblos.

a stamped design called the "bear paw." This pueblo also produces
highly polished red-on-red ware. Surface gloss of both the redware
and blackware is the result of long and painstaking rubbing. Incidentally, the clay used for blackware is red. It gets its black color by
being covered with ashes and other materials during the firing.

Picuris pots are brown, undecorated cooking ware. The clay used
contains innumerable gold-colored particles of mica which gives the
pottery a metallic glitter. Picuris pots are favorites of gourmets, who
claim that beans cooked in them have an authentic southwestern
flavor.

Zuñi pottery is thick-walled, and irregular in shape. One typical design motif is the deer. Zuñis also make jars in the form of owls. Pottery is dying out in Zuñi, as most people have turned to making jewelry, at which they can earn more money.

Hopi pottery differs from that of the other pueblos. Traditional abstract designs are painted on a dark cream or amber background. Hopi pottery exemplifies the influence one single talented and dedicated person can have on the development of art. A hundred years ago almost no pottery was made in Hopi villages. Then Nampeyo, a woman of Hano Pueblo, influenced by early pottery dug up in the

Maria of San Ildefonso, maybe the most famous of all Pueblo pottery makers, is credited with having invented the famous black-on-black ware.

Helen Cordero of Cochiti is widely known for her ceramic sculptures, especially the figure of a storyteller. "Some people imitate my work," she says, "but you can tell. The eyes of my figures are always slits. Those of my imitators are round dots."

ruins of an abandoned village, began to make pottery in the ancient style. Her example was followed by others, and in this way the art was revived among the Hopis.

Today, at Cochiti, Helen Cordero has carried the art of pottery one step further by creating ceramic sculptures for which she has become famous. Among her favorite subjects is the figure of an old-style storyteller surrounded by children.

Maybe the finest pottery today is made at Acoma. Acoma pots have the thinnest walls of all Pueblo ware. If tapped lightly, they have a high clear ring to them. They are meticulously made in the ancient Anasazi way, and their design is beautiful.

Here is how Santana Antonio makes her Acoma pottery. The clay is dug up high on the mesas from under large slabs of sedimentary rock. It cannot be used as is, but must be mixed with ground-up pieces of old, prehistoric pottery found in and around ruins. The clay of the potsherds acts as a bonding agent.

Another form of clay is the white slip or whitewash, which is used to cover the pot while still soft, before firing. It forms the background color on which the designs are painted. The colors used for the designs are black and a bright orange-red. They are made from natural rocks.

Tools needed to make pottery are stones—for grinding the old potsherds and the rocks. Brushes, made from thin yucca stalks flattened between the teeth and trimmed straight across, are used to paint on the designs. Scrapers are made from filed-down sardine cans, to thin the walls of pots to a uniform thickness. Smoothers are made from stiff slices of gourds cut into various shapes. A small pocket knife comes in handy for trimming the edges of pots.

The first step in making a pot is to soak and prepare the clay and powdered potsherds and mix them in the right proportion. Pots are formed from one big lump of clay or built up from many coils. Shaping starts by pushing the fingers into the clay, rotating it, and enlarging the hole. One hand turns the clay while the other shapes the inside walls. Smoothers and scrapers are then used on the outside until the pot takes the desired shape.

At this stage the hardened pot must be polished. This is often done

(1) Pottery making begins with the digging of the clay.

(2) A well-known pottery maker, Santana has to crush old pottery into a powder to add to the freshly dug clay. A pot made only with new clay might crack.

(3) As Santana works on her pottery her gra[n]children watch. Watching is fun and learni[ng] too.

# A POTTERY MAKER AT WORK

(4) Santana Antonio of Acoma shapes her pot in the manner of the ancient Anasazi—without a pottery wheel.

(5) Polished with stones, dried in the sun, whitewashed, and designs painted on, the pots are ready to be fired in a pit lined with pieces of dried cow dung.

with rounded pieces of jasper or agate called "gizzard stones." They got this name because it is believed that great amounts of these pebbles were swallowed, millions of years ago, by dinosaurs. Rubbing together in these fabled monsters' stomachs the gizzard stones helped to crush the vegetable matter that the dinosaur had swallowed for its food, thereby helping the creature's digestion. Now the stones help Pueblo women polish their pottery. After it is polished, the rim of the pot is trimmed and it is left in the sun to dry. When the drying is done the liquid slip, or whitewash, is applied with a rag. It dries very quickly and is immediately polished again. The pot is now ready for painting.

The design is painted on, usually the black color first. The patterns are not sketched out beforehand but controlled by memory, by the hand, and by the eye. The designs are almost always traditional ones that can be found on Anasazi pottery hundreds of years old.

Now comes the last and trickiest part: the firing. It is done in a pit lined with "chips"—dried pieces of cow or sheep dung. Large pieces of broken pottery are used to insulate the ceramics to be fired from the actual flames. The pots are then completely covered with broken pieces which in turn are covered with dry manure and then set on fire. The heat is intense—much hotter than burning wood. If during the firing one hears a loud "pop" or "bang," that is bad news for the potter. It means that a piece was not completely or evenly dried and has burst under the heat. The fire burns for about two or three hours. Finally the pit is uncovered and the finished pieces are revealed, gleaming, their colors heightened by the fire, a joy to behold. This is how an Acoma pot is made.

Pueblo pottery comes in all shapes: decorative pottery, twin wedding jars, water ollas, cooking pots, ashtrays. At Acoma very charming pottery toys are made in the shapes of animals or miniature pots. A few Acoma women also make ceramic necklaces.

Among the best-known works of the Pueblo artists are the so-

These kachina dolls have been made at Jemez; most of them, however, are carved in the Hopi villages.

called kachina dolls. *Kachina* is a Hopi word. It can mean godlike beings (Kachinas), or the dancers who impersonate these gods during ceremonies, or the dolls. There are over two hundred Hopi Kachinas, and for each one there is a doll. A kachina doll is not a sacred object. The dolls are given by the dancers to the children to familiarize the young with Hopi beliefs, and to teach them the meanings of the different masks. More and more kachina dolls are now made exclusively for Indian arts and crafts stores, to be bought by white collectors. These dolls are generally as authentic and meticulously made as those handed out by the masked dancers to Pueblo children. Most kachina dolls are carved from cottonwood tree roots. A pocket knife is used to block out the basic figure of the doll, and a piece of sandstone smoothes it. The figure is coated with an underpaint of white clay, the colors, nowadays mostly commercial poster colors, are applied. A fairly recent development are groups of kachina dolls representing a whole scene, such as a sacred clown climbing a pole, or a number of figurines performing the Hopi snake dance. Good kachina dolls are valuable, especially the older ones. If you are lucky enough to own one, treasure it.

One of the more recent Pueblo arts is making silver and turquoise jewelry. Body ornaments have been made of bone, stone, shells, and turquoise since prehistoric times, but today's Pueblo jewelry does not go back much farther than a hundred years. The Indians learned silversmithing from the Spaniards. By the 1890s most pueblos had at least a few men working at the craft. At first, silver jewelry was exclusively for home use. It soon became the fashion to wear a lot of jewelry on feast and ceremonial days. Soon the craft, the designs, and the materials used became part of Pueblo tradition. After the coming of the railroads and the tourists, more and more jewelry was sold to outsiders.

In the beginning the silver used came from coins—both American and Mexican. Turquoise was dug from ancient Indian mines. Nowadays the old sources are exhausted, and all raw materials are bought at trading stores.

Early Indian silver was hammered work with simple stamped or engraved ornaments. Later, the ornaments became more complicated. New techniques were invented, and electric tools were used. Pueblos developed their own specialties. Hopi silversmiths developed a style using plain silver decorated with old pottery designs. Santo Domingo jewelers became famous for their *hishis*—strands of finely drilled coral, turquoise, or shell beads. The most spectacular jewelry is made

At Zuñi there is a jewelry maker in almost every family. The young woman shown here is using bits of semiprecious stone to set into rings.

at Zuñi. The specialty of the village is highly intricate inlay work using turquoise, coral, jet, and mother-of-pearl in a profusion of designs—butterflies, dancing gods, thunderbirds, floral and snow-flake patterns. Everything is made at Zuni—rings, earrings, shell pendants, bracelets of clustered turquoise, and massive as well as thin and delicate necklaces. Formerly, jewelry was made entirely by men, but women in increasing numbers are busy at the craft which in some places has become a main source of income.

Two Zuñi crafts in one picture: a fine old pot and some exquisite silver and turquoise jewelry.

Finally, out of the ancient tradition of Pueblo crafts grew the modern Indian painting movement. Many of today's best-known Pueblo artists have been students of the famous U.S. Indian School at Santa Fe, New Mexico. Pueblo painters first exhibited in the 1930s. Among the early Pueblo artists were Mapewi and Ha-we-la-na of Zia, Awa Tsireh of San Ildefonso, and Chiu-Tah of Taos. Later, Hopi artists Raymond Naha and Fred Kabotie became famous for their fine paintings, as did Pablita Velarde of Santa Clara and José Rey

Toledo of Jemez, a U.S. health officer who, besides being an outstanding artist, is also a respected poet. Many of today's Pueblo painters use the techniques and imagery of modern art, but if you look closer you will recognize the forms and symbols of the ancient Anasazis.

Where can Pueblo art be bought? In the old days Pueblo craftsmen and women sold their wares directly to white travelers along the highways and at the local railroad station. Since the coming of the modern superhighways, selling along the road has been outlawed as a traffic hazard, and railroad stations are fewer and no longer important. Some selling in the open is, however, still done by Santo Domingo craftsmen on the main plaza in Sante Fe. Places to buy Pueblo crafts are tribal guild shops near Oraibi on the Hopi reservation, or at Zuñi. The Navajo tribal shop at Window Rock sells some Pueblo as well as Navajo crafts. Jewelry can be bought locally at Santo Domingo and Zuñi, pottery at Acoma, San Ildefonso, and Santa Clara. There are many Indian craft shops in Santa Fe, Taos, and Albuquerque, New Mexico, and in Tucson, Phoenix, and Scottsdale, Arizona.

It is always best to buy from the Indian artist—first, because the price is cheaper than in a store, and second, because the artist gets a little more money when there is no middleman. Do not buy pawned jewelry. I once saw a white woman boasting of having bought a squash-blossom necklace worth hundreds of dollars for a fraction of its cost from a pawnbroker. An Indian walked over and spit on her necklace. Rude, maybe, but not undeserved. Indians may have to pawn their treasures for grocery money and then be unable to redeem them. Buying their pawn is not necessarily cheap. A trader in Gallup puts his jewelry into a hock shop for a day, redeems it, and exhibits the pieces in his shop window with the pawn tags still attached. The unwary tourist thinks he is getting pawned items cheap at the expense of some poor Indian; in reality, he is paying an exorbitant price for his greed.

In many villages jewelry making is a main source of income.

Indian crafts have become fashionable, and prices have gone up. The Southwest is also full of cheap imitations manufactured in Europe and Asia, or even mass-produced in American factories. Rugs vaguely resembling Navajo rugs, are machine-woven in New England. Others, harder to distinguish from the real thing, are hand-loomed in Mexico. Coral beads of "genuine Santo Domingo *hishis*" are sometimes made of glass manufactured in Taiwan, and a turquoise necklace—gorgeous at a distance—can easily turn out to be plastic. Pottery, painted gaudily in poster or "Glo" colors, is not real, fired pottery. The color is not waterproof and will run or smear when wet. Take a close look before you buy. Enjoy your Indian crafts, but make sure they *are* Indian.

Though a few Pueblos were among the Indians who seized Wounded Knee in 1973, armed confrontation is not the way of the peaceful Pueblos. They prefer to fight for their rights in a court of law or in the court of public opinion.

# 14 ▪ THE NEW INVADERS

*Surely, the Great Spirit did not*
*intend for us to shrivel up and*
*die and our bones be scattered,*
*only to be remembered in anthropology*
*text books.*

FRANK TENORIO

Indians are "in" nowadays. They have caught the public eye and public sympathy. They have, in the last few years, won court case after court case—on paper. Thus, many people, even Native Americans, fail to see how much discrimination and injustice remain.

The picture presented on the following pages is one-sided. It represents the view of the Indian—conservative and activist, traditionalist and progressive. It is important to listen to them, to perceive them as persons, not as stereotypes who sing and dance, pose for a photograph in return for a half dollar, or try to sell you some pottery.

What the Indians try to tell us is that they are not racist. They try to get it across to us that they are not against the individual white man—whom they will often embrace as a close friend—but against the white society's system which oppresses them and, as they frequently point out, oppresses the Anglo too, even though he is unaware of it. Their fight, as they emphasize again and again, is not for themselves but for all of us.

Most Indians do not want to go back to dwell in caves or tipis and hunt with bow and arrows. They want to strike a sane balance between backwardness and overindustrialization which they consider as a great danger threatening the human race. While ready to accept some of the products of white culture and industry, they want to do so the Pueblo way, at their own pace, within the framework of their own life style. They do not want to join the rat race of a space-age society, which they say is no way to live. Rather would they persuade us to drop out of it. Above all, they want to remain themselves, to retain their language and customs and be masters of their own destiny. Increasingly Indians talk about "sovereignty," the right to rule themselves within their own reservations and pueblos without interference from Washington. It is in the context of this frame of mind that we should listen to the Pueblos' complaints.

Indian survival, and that includes Pueblo survival, may be threatened as never before. The new despoilers are not conquistadors in steel armor, mountain men with coonskin caps, or the U.S. Cavalry. The new invader is a polite man with a smile, a briefcase, a fountain pen, and a checkbook. He is the sometime unwitting agent of what one Indian leader called "the greatest ripoff in American history." The energy crisis and the need for new land to exploit commercially and industrially is sending an ever-swelling stream of speculators, businessmen, and corporate lawyers to Indian reservations and pueblos, which are among the few places left where natural resources are still up for grabs. And so, in years to come, Indians everywhere will face a crisis of major proportions. What are the problems facing the Pueblos in the immediate future?

New Mexico and Arizona are called "Lands of Enchantment," and "A Tourist's Paradise," but how many tourists are aware of the grimmer picture that cannot be seen from a car or a motel balcony? There is, first, a basic threat to physical survival. Said one Indian leader in Farmington: "For years, it has been almost a sport, a sort of sick, perverted tradition among Anglo youths . . . to go into the Indian section of town and physically assault and rob elderly and sometimes intoxicated men and women, for no apparent reason other than that they were Indians." At Farmington Indian men were slain, seemingly just for the fun of it. The victims were Navajos. In other

The new white conquerors are developers, the coal company men, the seekers of raw materials. This giant machine is part of a strip-mining operation at Black Mesa, Arizona; it is despoiling the land of the Hopis and Navajos.

places, such as in Gallup, sober, non-drinking Pueblos were killed. In the spring of 1971 the bodies of two Zuñi men and one other unidentified Indian were found with numerous stab wounds, victims of those who "would walk a mile just to kill an Indian."

These extreme cases are undoubtedly rare, but Indians are victims of many forms of racism. Besides, there are other ways of killing a people than with a gun or knife. The Indian's average life span is

Indians feel insulted by this kind of exploitative advertising with which
white traders try to attract tourists.

still around forty-five years, over twenty years less than that of white
Americans. Pueblos still die of diseases that, by and large, have been
conquered in white communities. Health problems arise just by eating the white man's food. A scientist at the University of New Mexico
stated that malnutrition among Pueblos would be no problem if
Indians ate their traditional native foods: "Our studies found that
Indian native foods, when consumed in their natural form, such as
kernels of corn, bleached with lime and ground to make tortillas or
bread, are quite nutritional. . . . It is when these foods are commer-
cialized, or when the Indians desert their indigenous staples for con-

venience foods, that the nutritional values go way down and health suffers."

A Jemez Indian commented: "Hunger comes from lack of money. Lack of money comes from lack of jobs. Lack of jobs comes from racism and discrimination. We would like to feed ourselves in the old way, but in some pueblos this is no longer possible because of shrinking acres and increasing population. Formerly we could roam far and wide to hunt, or to gather pine nuts. Now we are restricted to the borders of our reservations, borders drawn up by the white man. Lands where deer once browsed and pine trees grew are now cities and highways. Life is difficult and we must be ever watchful."

Bodies might be safe and well fed, but the spirit might be killed. Adi Defender, a woman from Jemez remembers: "As soon as I entered the gates of the government day school I was forbidden to speak my mother tongue. If I did, and of course I did, I ended up writing on the blackboard and several sheets of paper: *I will not talk Indian.*" Adi Defender also remembers teachers at the mission school egging on white pupils to call her "a litte red devil." She also spoke of how irrelevant the teaching was, with textbook stories about offices and helicopters, or illustrations of umbrellas or subways—"things we had never seen or heard about." As one tribal chairman said: "Every time someone says how good we are with our hands, I want to ask, 'Why not give us the chance to show what we can do with our minds?'"

One struggle of Pueblo men and women today is to gain control of, or at least a voice in, their children's schools. They want to have a say in the curriculum and the way it is taught. They want the jobs in and around the pueblos, in the Bureau of Indian Affairs, or in the Indian Health Service to go to Indians. They also want traders and their stores to charge Indians no more than white people for the same items, to pay them fairly for their arts and crafts, and not to overcharge them on raw materials or loans.

"We are the earth and the fire, the water and the wind," say the Indians. Land and man are one. Take the one and you kill the other. More than ever, the Pueblos have to fight for their land. In many places Indians are evicted as "squatters" from land that they have lived on for generations because the white boundaries are so drawn that it no longer belongs to them. The National Indian Youth Council, whose headquarters are at Albuquerque, in Pueblo land, commented: "We are increasingly disturbed at proposals in the Bureau of Land Management to evict Indian people from their ancestral homes. People living on certain lands for scores of years are now told that this land is no longer theirs due to a new BLM survey. We are amazed at the audacity of the federal government, after stealing an entire country, to now try to force Indian people off the few acres they have left. The clear reason the BLM wants to retain the land is that it wishes to lease out the land to strip-mining companies. Again, Indian people are being forced to sacrifice their land and their livelihood to bail out the white man from his wasteful expenditure of energy. The Bureau of Land Management, by its statement that 'trespassers' will have to leave, shows that it puts material values over human values."

Worse are direct attacks on Pueblo reservation land often disguised as "business deals." At Cochiti the Army Corps of Engineers built a dam, made an artificial lake, and around it, on 7500 acres of tribal land, leased for 99 years, a new white luxury city is rising. Street names are Indian. One is Shrotsem Street; it means "I love you" in Keresan. The land sells for up to $12,500 per lot, and the developers grow rich. There are townhouses, residential homes, and ranchettes; a shopping center with Muzak; recreational areas with tennis courts, golf, swimming, and horseback riding; a "pueblo-style" Levittown with plastic plants; interiors with vinyl zebra-print couches; and saleswomen dressed in moccasins, beaded headbands, turquoise necklaces, and bracelets. The new white Cochiti is adver-

By white standards, most Pueblos are poor. Their income, on the average, is only half of what white Americans earn. Much of their housing is substandard.

tised as "The Land of Seven-day Weekends." Blurbs read: "Find arrowheads in your back yard" and "See the colorful dances held annually." Another brochure has the headline: *Watch a lake happen!*

Leasing the land and thereby possibly losing it forever has divided the pueblo. Some families have emigrated to Santo Domingo. Says Sam Arquero: "You know, I really resent environmentalists coming out here and telling us not to build. Why should they tell us what to do? *They are eating!* We weren't tricked into signing that contract. You think we like this? I don't like them coming up here and putting up these houses. They are a threat to our Indian culture." But the people of Cochiti were poor and the payments offered them too much of a temptation.

A little ways north of Santa Fe, near Tesuque pueblo, stands a peeling, already fading billboard: *Colonias de Santa Fe Now Offering Home Sites. A master-planned community. Sales office representative on duty.* But do not look for the salesman; he is no longer there. In 1968 the federal Indian Land Law was amended, after some lobbying by certain interested parties, to permit 99-year leasing of specified Indian lands. In 1970 Tesuque Pueblo signed a 99-year land lease with Sangre de Cristo Development Company, the parent of Colonias de Santa Fe, to create a white community of recreational homes and high-rise apartments. In 1971 promotion and lot sales began. In 1972 the project was suspended indefinitely. According to local newspapers fraud was alleged, and involvement with a "shady, mafia-connected figure" in the land-promotion business. Federal officials, charged with protecting Indian interests, washed their hands of the whole deal saying that "it was strictly a private matter between the tribe and the speculators." In 1972 the people of Tesuque filed suit seeking cancellation of the 99-year lease of 5400 acres of their small pueblo. They also charged the government with a breach of its trust responsibilities. Indians throughout the Southwest called the deal an "attempted massive land and water ripoff." Today the project seems almost dead, though there are those—politicians and money men—who would like to revive it. The fight of the Tesuque people for their land is by no means over.

*Akwesasne Notes* headlined the story: *Our land—their future.* A government official said unofficially, "What's good for the Bureau of Reclamation, is good for the Department of the Interior, is good for New Mexico, is good for you and me." But, you and me does not include Indians.

A lawyer said, "Many Pueblos lack sophisticated knowledge of their rights and how to get them."

It is not only the land the men with the briefcases are after, but the minerals in the land. At Laguna it is uranium. "The great corporate monster, Anaconda, is still digging a big hole in the ground. You can see the grey dirt piled so high, miles of it. Snow Covered Peak is being turned inside out. The hole right to the east of Pajuate village is getting bigger and ever bigger, and the people are afraid that the old village will one day soon collapse into the hole. A lot of guys work there, and even though they see one part of their life and community being destroyed, what the Hell can they do? It's good pay and all. The monster's geologists and engineers keep on digging," one Indian writes. The mining company, no doubt, would point out that their operations provide much needed income for the pueblo. Everywhere the fight for the land continues, and will continue for a long time. Sometimes, the Indians are winning. In 1972 the government returned the Sacred Blue Lake and more than 30,000 acres to the pueblo of Taos, but for every victory there is a defeat.

Land is nothing without water. At Tesuque, Cochiti, and elsewhere, the land developers are eager to secure rights "to sink and drill wells" in places where there is hardly enough water for the Pueblos to irrigate their own corn patches. Indian water is diverted everywhere to serve Anglo needs. As one lawyer said, "Pueblo water is flowing from a number of reservations to the toilets and fountains of Albuquerque, Santa Fe, Los Angeles and Salt Lake City."

Frank Tenorio, of San Felipe Pueblo, testified, "In a way I might be termed a hematologist. This is a medical doctor who concerns himself with problems of the blood. For indeed water is the blood of the Pueblo people. There has been a lot said about the sacredness of our land which is our body; and the value of our culture which is our soul; but, if the blood of our people stops its life-giving flow or becomes polluted, all else will die and the many thousands of years of our communal existence will come to an end.

"Our old enemies the Anglos and the Spanish have now settled around us. They will not give back to use what they have stolen, but we have survived them. But we now face our greatest enemies. They do not go by the names of Coronado, or Cortez, or Custer, but by the name of Army Corps of Engineers, San Juan-Chama Diversion Project, Salt River Project, and so forth. In facing these new adversaries who threaten our existence I now know how my Pueblo brothers who had passed on felt when they stood on the rooftops of their pueblos and saw for the first time these people with white skin with shining armor shooting fire out of sticks and logs which were killing their people and destroying their homes. We learned their powers and we survived them. We will also learn the ways of all our adversaries who now hide behind such initials as BIA and BLM and we will survive them too."

At Black Mesa water is taken from the Navajos and the Hopis, to be used in the strip-mining process "to help solve the nation's energy crisis." The eastern pueblos of Pojoaque, Tesuque, Nambe and San Ildefonso see their water drained off for the use of whites. "The government," says one San Ildefonso elder, "is a Jekyll and Hyde, trying to protect us and steal from us at the same time." Right is on the Indian side, but justice is smothered, as one lawyer says: "by deliberate obscurantism, under tons of red tape, megatons of legalistic double-talk and nit-picking."

A main cause for the frantic search for ever more land and water are, of course, the developers trying to make New Mexico into a new Florida—a land of recreational communities and condominiums attracting multitudes of buyers looking for "nice retirement opportunities." As Frank Tenorio, chairman of the Water Rights Committee of the All-Indian Pueblo Council, puts it, "Since they are making a sardine can out of New Mexico, maybe they can provide soybean oil to preserve the people since they don't have the water to do it."

Says Benny Atencio of Santo Domingo, "As Pueblo Indians we do not recognize the theory that our rights to water and other natural resources can be limited, or restricted, or taken away from us by any state or its citizens. Our rights to the water have always been inherent in our land base. The non-Indians cannot come into our reservations or homes and begin to dictate to the American Indian his destiny and pursuit of life, but they are trying." As one land management official remarked, off the record, "Whoever is willing and able to pay the most for the water will get it, and that won't be the Indian." And so the competition for the Pueblo's lifeblood continues.

If his religion and his culture are the Indian's soul, then the soul, too, is the subject of attacks. A missionary newsletter from the Hopi Bible School in Polacca read in part:

Pray for Mishongnovi, a Hopi village steeped in witchcraft. Many people feel the Indian dances are for show and entertainment. If you are ever near one of these dances, you can feel the very presence of evil forces as they actually worship the devil. This is in the United States! Will you help us pray? There are few Christians in this village, and oh what persecution they suffer. If enough Christian people would ban together, we could bind the forces of evil and claim this village for Jesus!

If this had been written in 1900, it would have been what one could expect. But, incredibly, it was written in the 1970s.

A few years ago a Pueblo medicine man or priest was arrested and jailed for draft evasion. He was not given the same rights as a white clergyman because his Indian belief was not recognized as a religion.

The Pueblo's religion is further desecrated by fake ceremonials staged to rake in tourists dollars. But the Pueblos are fighting back. In 1969 Indians filed suit against the Gallup Ceremonial Association for violating the civil rights of three Indian students who were forcibly prevented from distributing leaflets among the spectators and participants. The leaflet read in part:

When our grandfathers carried guns, they were free and they were people. The Anglos had to reckon with them and were careful not to anger our people. Our grandfathers stood up for what they felt was right and condemned what they knew was wrong. If we Indians of today were like our grandfathers, we would not allow this ceremonial to be held year after year in this manner and in this place.

Just because Indians sing and dance for you, that does not mean they are happy. The City of Gallup calls the Ceremonial "A Tribute to the American Indian." Do not believe it! Do not think that Gallup respects the Indians because it gives them a free barbecue.

Do not let the Ceremonial let you forget that Indians have the highest unemployment rate, the highest infant mortality rate in this country, the lowest average income of any group in the United States, the highest drop-out rate, and don't forget that many Indians you see suffer from malnutrition.

You should also ask yourself why the Ceremonial is held to benefit the City of Gallup. Ask yourself why Indians are not in charge of the Ceremonial. Ask yourself why the Ceremonial is not moved to an Indian reservation, since there are so many of them in the area. If you are brave enough to see what the City of Gallup thinks of the Indian find out where the Gallup Indian Community Center is located and see it for yourself. Note that it is dirty and in need of repair. In a study made of the economy of Gallup, it was learned that 72% of the business was carried on with Indians as customers. It was also learned that the merchants of Gallup contribute very little to the Indian Center. Gallup provides little in the way of public services to the Indian.

The city policemen are seen many times savagely beating helpless drunk Indians. But Gallup continues calling itself the "Indian Capital of the World." Recently, Gallup decided it needed a flag. Most of the entries so far made use of Indian designs and figures and most were designed by non-Indians. The Ceremonial is only one example of how Gallup capitalizes on the Indian. . . . You will ask: "Why don't they protest?" As you look at the Indians dance and sing for you, say to yourself: "They were people . . . when their grandfathers had guns."

Protests have eroded the Ceremonial. By 1974 only half as many Indians as before came to participate, and their parade had to be protected by a screen of helmeted police. An elder from Jemez Pueblo spoke, "We must act with dignity, as Indians, as human

In the 1970s, Pueblos, Navajos, and other southwestern tribes have been demonstrating at Gallup, New Mexico, against discrimination, brutal abuse of Native Americans, and the desecration of sacred dances for the amusement of white tourists.

persons, to let Gallup know, to let New Mexico know. We are here for all humanity." Clearly the great ceremonial Indian "Song and Dance Doin's" are no longer what they were only a few years ago.

I have spoken about the Pueblo's way of life. I have described it as once lived and as still lived in many places. The descriptions have, I am sure, often led to an image of idyllic, romantic, mysterious and enchanted pueblos. And there is something to this image which has for so many years charmed and fascinated the white visitor. But it is a partial picture only, and it would be wrong to hide the fierce struggles which the peaceful Pueblos, as well as other tribes, have to wage, day in and day out, for their existence. The Pueblos are fighting back on many fronts. They are fighting back as individuals, as tribes, and as a group through the All-Indian Pueblo Council. They are fighting with the help of other Indian and sometimes non-Indian organizations.

For the first time Hopis, who have never recognized the jurisdiction of either the U.S. government or the white courts, are suing this government as well as private corporations as well as individuals. Everywhere Pueblos are vigorously defending their land, their environment, their water, and their rights as people. They are not overlooking symbolic gestures which have much meaning for them. They are debunking the great white heroes who "won the West."

In 1974, for instance, Taos veterans protested the name of nearby Kit Carson Memorial State Park and asked that it be renamed for Santiago "Jimmy" Lujan, a Taos GI who during World War II died in a Japanese prisoner-of-war camp. They were protesting against the whole Kit Carson cult, the cult of the all-powerful, John Wayne-type white conqueror, against the many Kit Carson parks, streets, plazas, statues, and memorials. They carried a poster: *Kit Carson Was a Tramp*. They pointed out that his massacre of Navajos and his driving out of the survivors from their ancestral lands on the infamous "March of Death" was not different from My Lai or Auschwitz. They were refused a permit to march in the Taos town square or in the annual Taos Fiesta. On the other hand, someone stole up to the thirty-foot high statue of Kit Carson in Santa Fe and did some chiseling. An inscription at the statue's base hailed Carson as the Conqueror of savage races. One day it was found that the word "savage" had been chipped away.

A policy statement of the National Indian Youth Council well expresses what the Pueblos want and think:

We are the products of the poverty, despair, and discrimination pushed on our people from the outside. We are products of chaos. Chaos in our tribes. Chaos in our personal lives.

We are also products of a rich and ancient culture which supercedes and makes bearable any oppressions we are forced to bear. We believe that one's basic identity should be with his tribe. We believe in tribalism, we believe that tribalism is what has caused us to endure.

The protection of our land and water and other natural resources are of utmost importance to us. Our culture not only exists in time but in space as well. If we lose our land we are adrift like a leaf on a lake, which will float aimlessly and then dissolve and disappear.

Our land is more than the ground upon which we stand and sleep, and in which we bury our dead. The land is our spiritual mother whom we can no easier sell than our physical mother. We will resist, to the death if necessary, any more of our mother being sold into slavery.

Survival of Indians as a people means the survival of Indians as a community. A community is the interdependence of Indian people from which flows our religion and our sense of well-being. We affirm the tribal community as a workable and satisfying way to survive in this and other centuries. The wisdom of living this way for thousands of years has taught us this.

An ancient Anasazi could not have stated it better.

# BIBLIOGRAPHY

Bahti, Tom. *Southwestern Indian Tribes*. KC Publications, 1968.

Bahti, Tom. *Southwestern Indian Ceremonials*. KC publications, 1970.

Bandelier, Adolf F. *The Delight Makers*. New York: Dodd, Mead, 1960.

Benedict, Ruth. *Patterns of Culture*. Boston: Houghton Mifflin Company, 1943.

Ceram, C. W. *The First Americans*. New York: Harcourt, Brace Jovanovich, 1971.

Clissold, Stephen. *The Seven Cities of Cibola*. New York: Clarkson N. Potter, 1961.

Cushing, Frank Hamilton. *Zuni Folk Tales*. New York: G. P. Putnam's Sons, 1901.

De Benavides, Alonso. *The Memorial of Fray Alonso de Benavides*. Chicago: University of Chicago Press, 1916.

Dockstader, Frederic, J. *The Kachina and the White Man*. Cranbrook Institute of Science, 1954.

Dozier, Edward P. *The Pueblo Indians of North America*. New York: Holt, Rinehart and Winston, 1970.

Fergusson, Erna. *Dancing Gods*. Albuquerque: University of New Mexico Press, 1931.

Fergusson, Erna. *Our Southwest*. New York: Alfred A. Knopf, 1940.

Fergusson, Erna. *New Mexico*. New York: Alfred A. Knopf, 1964.

Forrest, Earle R. *The Snake Dance of the Hopi Indians*. Westernlore Press, 1961.

Goddard, Pliny Earle. *Indians of the Southwest*. New York: American Museum of Natural History, 1931.

Gregg, Josiah. *Commerce of the Prairies*. Tulsa: University of Oklahoma Press, 1954.

Hall-Quest, Olga. *Conquistadors and Pueblos*. New York: E. P. Dutton, 1969.

Horgan, Paul. *Great River: The Rio Grande*. New York: Holt, Rinehart and Winston, 1954.

Horgan, Paul. *Conquistadors in North America*. New York: Macmillan, 1963.

274

James, George Wharton. *The Indians of the Painted Desert Region.* Boston: Little, Brown, 1903.

Jennings, Jesse D. and Edward Norbeck. *Prehistoric Men in the New World.* Chicago: University of Chicago Press, 1964.

Jones, Oakah L. *Pueblo Warriors.* Tulsa: University of Oklahoma Press, 1954.

Josephy, Alvin M., Jr. *The Indian Heritage of America.* New York: Alfred A. Knopf, 1968.

Kidder, Alfred Vincent. *An Introduction to the Study of Southwestern Archaelogy.* New Haven, Conn.: Yale University Press, 1962.

Kluckhohn, Clyde. *To the Foot of the Rainbow.* New York: Century Company, 1927.

Lummis, Charles F. *Some Strange Corners of Our Country.* New York: Century Company, 1901.

Lummis, Charles F. *The Land of Poco Tiempo.* New York: Charles Scribner's Sons, 1906.

Lummis, Charles F. *Mesa, Cañon and Pueblo.* New York: Century Company, 1925.

Marriot, Alice. *Maria, the Potter of San Ildefonso.* Tulsa: University of Oklahoma Press, 1948.

Martin, Paul S. *Indians Before Columbus.* Chicago: University of Chicago Press, 1947.

McNickle, D'Arcy. *Indian Tribes of the United States.* New York: Oxford University Press, 1962.

McNitt, Frank. *Richard Wetherill: Anasazi.* Albuquerque: University of New Mexico Press, 1957.

Ortiz, Alfonso. *The World of the Tewa Indians.* Chicago: University of Chicago Press, 1969.

Robinson, Will H. *Under Turquoise Skies.* New York: Macmillan, 1928.

Sedgewick, Mrs. William T. *Acoma, The Sky City.* Rio Grande Press, 1927.

Silverberg, Robert. *The Old Ones.* New York: New York Graphic Society, 1965.

Simpson, Ruth De Ette. *The Hopi Indians.* Southwest Museum Leaflets, 1953.

Spicer, Edward H. *Cycles of Conquest.* Phoenix: University of Arizona Press, 1962.

Talayeswa, Don. *Sun Chief: The Autobiography of a Hopi Indian*. New Haven, Conn.: Yale University Press, 1942.

Terrel, John Upton. *Pueblos, Gods and Spaniards*. New York: Dial Press, 1973.

Underhill, Ruth. *Pueblo Crafts*. Washington, D.C.: U.S. Department of the Interior, 1944.

Underhill, Ruth. *Workaday Life of the Pueblos*. Washington, D.C.: United States Indian Service, 1946.

Underhill, Ruth. *The Red Man's Religion*. Chicago: University of Chicago Press, 1965.

Waters, Frank. *The Man Who Killed the Deer*. London: Neville Spearman, 1942.

Waters, Frank. *Masked Gods*. Denver: Swallow Press, 1950.

Waters, Frank, and Fredericks, Oswald White Bear. *Book of the Hopi*. New York: Viking Press, 1963.

Watson, Don. *Indians of the Mesa Verde*. Mesa Verde Museum Association, 1961.

Weaver, Thomas. *Indians of Arizona*. Phoenix: University of Arizona Press, 1974.

White, Leslie A. *The Acoma Indians*. Rio Grande Press Reprint, 1973.

Wormington, H. M. *Prehistoric Indians of the Southwest*. Denver: Denver Museum of Natural History, 1964.

# INDEX

**Richard Erdoes**, artist, photographer, and writer, is the author of *The Sun Dance People, Lame Deer, Seeker of Vision*, and two soon-to-be published books about the Indian civil rights movement. An ardent supporter of Indian civil rights and an unofficial advisor to AIM, Richard Erdoes has been actively involved in Indian causes since a *Life* assignment took him west in 1953. Since then he is always found where the action is. He was at Wounded Knee, while his apartment in New York City became the eastern headquarters of that famous struggle. He was at the Bureau of Indian Affairs in Washington when it was taken over to dramatize the Trail of Broken Treaties. He and his family were with their Indian friends at Mount Rushmore to demand the return of The Sacred Black Hills to the Sioux Indians. A friend of many Indian leaders, Richard Erdoes is known and respected by Indian tribes throughout the country. He lives in New York with his wife, Jean, also a painter, in an apartment full of Indian art.